INSIGHT COMPACT GUIDE

P

C000260945

Compact Guide: Paris is the ultimate quick-reference guide to the French capital. It tells you all you need to know about the attractions of the city, from the soaring Eiffel Tower to the world-renowned collection of the Louvre, the majestic Notre-Dame and the eternally chic Left Bank.

This is one of 133 Compact Guides, combining the interests and enthusiasms of two of the world's best-known information providers: Insight Guides, whose innovative titles have set the standard for visual travel guides since 1970, and Discovery Channel, the world's premier source of nonfiction television programming.

APA PUBLICATIONS
Part of the Langenscheidt Publishing Group

L

Insight Compact Guide: Paris

Written by: Jack-Harry Back
English version by: David Ingram
Revised by: Isabelle Cornu and Clare Peel
Designed by: Clare Peel
Photography by: Jerry Denis/APA
Additional photography: Apa/Berlitz 21b, 24, 48, 76, 78; Pete Bennett 4r, 23b, 80b, 94b, 100; Britta Jaschinski 10t, 12b, 13, 16/17, 38b, 41, 60t, 60b, 65t, 68t, 68b, 69, 73t, 79t, 86, 115; Annabel Elston 4c, 5br, 21b, 44, 90b, 93; Jay Fechtman 121; AKG-images London/Erich Lessing 71t; AKG-images London 80t; The Art Archive 34, 35t, 35b, 54b, 79b, 97, 102b, 103; Bettmann/ Corbis 62; Bridgeman Art Library 95; Bridgeman Art Library/Musée Saint-Denis, Reims 23t; Bridgeman Art Library/Louvre, Paris 33; Bridgeman Art Library/Peter Willi 102t; Courtesy of the French Embassy 43, 91; Image Works/TopFoto 88; Musée Association Les Amis d'Edith Piaf 107; Courtesy of the Musée de la Mode et du Costume, Paris 56t; P.M.V.P. (Photothèque des Musées de la Ville de Paris) 82t; Courtesy of the Musée de Montmartre, Paris 85t; Ronald Grant Archive 26
Cover picture by: Powerstock
Picture Editor: Hilary Genin
Maps: Maria Randell/Laura Morris

Editorial Director: Brian Bell
Managing Editor: Clare Peel

CONTACTING THE EDITORS: As every effort is made to provide accurate information in this publication, we would appreciate it if readers would call our attention to any errors and omissions by contacting:
Apa Publications, PO Box 7910, London SE1 1WE, England.
Fax: (44 20) 7403 0290; e-mail: insight@apaguide.co.uk

Information has been obtained from sources believed to be reliable, but its accuracy and completeness, and the opinions based thereon, are not guaranteed.

© 2003 APA Publications GmbH & Co. Verlag KG Singapore Branch, Singapore.

First Edition 1995; second edition 1997; third edition 2003
Printed in Singapore by Insight Print Services (Pte) Ltd
Original edition © Polyglott-Verlag Dr Bolte KG, Munich

Distributed in the UK & Ireland by:
GeoCenter International Ltd
The Viables Centre, Harrow Way, Basingstoke,
Hampshire RG22 4BJ
Tel: (44 1256) 817-987, Fax: (44 1256) 817-988

Distributed in the United States by:
Langenscheidt Publishers, Inc.
46–35 54th Road, Maspeth, NY 11378
Tel: (1 718) 784-0055, Fax: (1 718) 784-0640

Worldwide distribution enquiries:
APA Publications GmbH & Co. Verlag KG (Singapore Branch)
38 Joo Koon Road, Singapore 628990
Tel: (65) 6865-1600, Fax: (65) 6861-6438

www.insightguides.com

PaRIS

Introduction

Places

Culture

Practical Information

▷ **Grande Arche (p46)** This monumental gate was one of President Mitterrand's 'grands projets', which took Paris to the cutting-edge of late 20th-century architecture.

▽ **Arc de Triomphe (p43)** Built in honour of Napoleon's victories, this arch dominates the eastern end of the Champs-Elysées.

△ **St-Germain and the Left Bank (p58)** Make like Sartre and De Beauvoir and drink coffee and philosophize in a Left Bank café – the epitome of Parisian intellectual life.

▽ **Notre-Dame (p24)** Located in the heart of Paris, on the romantic Ile de la Cité, is this monument to Catholicism and the great Gothic architects.

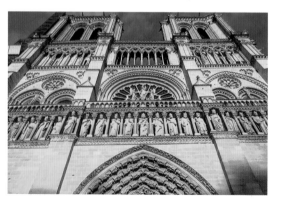

△ **Musée d'Orsay (p52)** Fine art from 1848 to 1919, most noted for its outstanding collection of Impressionist works.

▷ **Centre Pompidou (p75)** This inside-out behemoth showcases art from 1905 to the present: Klein, Matisse, Warhol, Miró, and so much more.

△ **The Louvre (p30)**
From the home of kings to forum for one of the world's best collections of fine and decorative arts.

▷ **Sainte-Chapelle (p19)** Louis IX wanted a shrine worthy of housing holy relics collected on his travels. The glorious Sainte-Chapelle's upper chapel, with its exquisite stained-glass windows, was the result.

△ **Montmartre (p84)**
Entertainment centre and home to the Sacré-Coeur — it's worth the climb up this most famous of hills.

◁ **Eiffel Tower (p47)**
Built for the 1889 World Fair, Gustave Eiffel's mighty iron monolith is still one of the most enduring symbols of Paris.

The Glory of France

'Paris', as the Emperor Charles V once said, 'is not a city, it is a world.'

Conquering the nation's capital was always uppermost in the minds of all the powers who warred with France over the centuries. Nor is this enduring love affair with Paris limited to emperors and kings; for centuries, painters, sculptors, composers and writers have been drawn to this glorious city. 'If you are lucky enough to have lived in Paris as a young man, then wherever you go for the rest of your life, it stays with you, for Paris is a moveable feast,' wrote American Francophile Ernest Hemingway.

BEYOND THE CLICHES

Many clichés are used to describe this enduringly appealing city: 'Paris, city of lovers', 'Paris, city of night-life', 'Paris, city of painters'. Certainly, the city's notorious *savoir vivre* still applies today, but the Paris behind the tourist façade is still a sprawling metropolis like any other, facing political, economic, social and cultural difficulties that are often enormously complex. For all its splendour, palatial building and excesses, there is always poverty and hardship. Yet both extremes are intimately connected with this city in their different ways.

BEST FOOT FORWARD

The most effective way of really getting a feel for Paris is to tread the city's pavements. Each of the different areas – or *quartiers* – has its own particular atmosphere. New perspectives open up wherever you go: elegant apartment buildings with magnificent façades on the one hand; ramshackle tenement blocks on the other. Parisian life is played out in the city's rear courtyards, tiny bistros, narrow streets, its elegant squares and, during the evenings, along the quays of the Seine – these are the places where the contrasts blend into one another.

> **Patron saint of Paris**
> *Circa* 451 Attila the Hun was preparing to invade Paris with his armies. The locals were ready to flee, but were prevented from doing so by a 19-year-old from Nanterre, called Geneviève. The pious girl predicted that the Huns would not harm the city, as long as the Parisians stayed with her and prayed. True enough, the invaders passed southwest of the city, only to be stopped in their tracks by an army of legionnaires. Geneviève was proclaimed the saviour of Paris.

Opposite: the Louvre pyramid
Below: the view of the city from Montmartre's Sacré-Coeur

LOCATION AND SIZE

Paris lies on roughly the same latitude as Stuttgart in Germany and Vancouver in Canada, at 2°20'east and 48°50' north. In terms of surface area, central Paris covers just 105sq km (40sq miles), which is relatively compact compared with many of the world's other capitals. The city boundary is approximately 36km (22 miles) long, and the distance from west to east (from Porte Maillot to Porte de Vincennes) is 12km (7 miles); from north to south (ie. from Porte de Clignancourt to Porte d'Orléans), the city measures nearly 10km (6 miles). The Greater Paris conurbation covers approximately 2,300sq km (890sq miles).

The city of Paris is contained within the Paris-Ile de France region (the equivalent of an English county). Covering an area of 12,000sq km (4,640sq miles), Paris-Ile de France consists of the Greater Paris conurbation as well as the *départements* (regional administrative districts) of Hauts-de-Seine, Val-de-Marne, Essonne, Seine-et-Marne, Seine-Saint-Denis, Val-d'Oise and Yvelines. This catchment area is almost exactly the same size as the US state of Connecticut.

Along the River Seine

THE CITY

Paris extends from the banks of the Seine up to the chain of hills in the north known as Butte Montmartre (*butte* means hill) and Butte Ste-Geneviève in the south. The city's elevation varies between roughly 25m (85ft) at Grenelle and 130m (425ft) at the top of Montmartre. In the city centre and to the east, there is very little distinction between office and residential areas – even large office blocks contain private apartments in their upper storeys. The suburbs located to the west and southwest are purely residential, however.

The city is intersected by two large series of streets. Forming a long line from north to south are the boulevard de Strasbourg, boulevard Sébastopol, boulevard du Palais and boulevard St-Michel. The east–west axis is made up of the rue du Faubourg St-Antoine, rue de Rivoli, avenue des Champs-Elysées and the avenue de la Grande Armée.

Vast reorganisation of Paris took place during the mid-19th century under Napoleon III and his legendary Prefect Baron Georges Haussmann, who gutted and rebuilt the city centre, creating Paris as we know it today. New water mains and a sewage system were installed to service the two million inhabitants of the capital. The elegant boulevards (known as the 'grands boulevards'), avenues and squares created at this time include the Champs-Elysées, the boulevards St-Michel and Saint-Gemain, and the vast star-shaped place de l'Etoile, home to the Arc de Triomphe. This vast reorganisation was not made solely for aesthetic reasons: it was also intended to facilitate swift deployment of troops in the event of riot or invasion.

> **The Parisian**
> 'The Parisian is interested in everything and, in the end, interested in nothing...Intoxicated as he is with something new from one day to the next, the Parisian, regardless of age, lives like a child. He complains of everything, tolerates everything, mocks everything, forgets everything, desires everything, tastes everything, feels everything passionately, drops everything casually – his kings, his conquests, his glory, his idol...'
> Writer, Honoré de Balzac

THE SEINE

Cutting Paris into two unequal halves – the *rive droite* (the right bank, north of the river) and the *rive gauche* (the left bank, south of the river) – is the meandering River Seine, which, at 765km (475 miles), is the longest river in Northern France. At the centre of the river are two islands, the Ile de la Cité and its diminutive

Retro covers

*Below: the shaded arches
of the rue de Rivoli
Bottom: literary St-Germain*

neighbour, the Ile Saint-Louis, while to the west of the city, near Passy, is another island, the narrow Ile des Cygnes. The Seine's two banks are connected by 37 bridges in the metropolitan area. The river reaches Paris close to the Bois de Vincennes, just after its confluence with the River Marne. The many moorings for its traffic lie between the Pont National and the Pont d'Austerlitz.

The Pont d'Austerlitz is also the starting-point for the Canal St-Martin, which leads off to the industrial areas in the east. The canal begins at the yacht harbour of Bassin de l'Arsénal, starts off underground, and connects with the harbour of Bassin de la Villette in the 19th *arrondissement*. The latter is connected to the Seine north of Paris by the 6.6-km (4-mile) long Canal St-Denis, and to the Marne via the 10.8-km (7-mile) long Canal de l'Ourcq.

CLIMATE

The climate in Paris is not dissimilar, although more extreme, than that in the south of England. Winter temperatures in Paris average 4°C (39°F), while summer temperatures occasionally hit 30°C (86°F); spring and autumn tend to be mild, with an average temperature of 11°C (52°F). June, September and October are the ideal months for

visiting in terms of climate, as they are warm, usually sunny, but less stifling (and crowded) than
the mid-summer months.

POPULATION

With a population of around 3 million (not including its suburbs), Paris is the seventh-largest city
in Europe. Roughly 12 million people – about one
fifth of the French population – live in the whole
Ile de France region. Here, the population density
is around 850 people per square kilometre (2,200
per square mile), but within Paris itself the figure
is as high as 25,000 per square kilometre (65,000
per square mile), making it the most densely populated city in Europe. Despite these figures, however, the population of Paris has been decreasing
in recent years due to dramatic rises in rents.

A national survey carried out in the late 1990s
put Parisians right at the top of the list of the most
hated people in France (31 percent), easily top-
ping traditional targets such as civil servants
(21 percent), Corsicans (23 percent) and even
policemen (18 percent). Much of this is doubtless
due to the famed arrogance of the Parisians,
who have long considered themselves to be
privvy to the best of France in every respect, from
culture and style to job opportunities and government activity.

However, as France becomes increasingly
decentralised, attitudes about the Parisians are
changing. The Paris press is full of stories about
stressed-out Parisians downsizing and moving out
in order to enjoy a better quality of life in the
countryside. A provincial coming to Paris today
no longer hides his or her regional accent when
looking for a job, and many now take pride in having such an accent.

Aside from the provinces, the largest contrib-
utors to the Parisian cultural and racial *pot au
feu* are the former colonies of West and North
Africa. Other earlier waves of immigration have
brought an influx of Chinese, Vietnamese, Poles,
Russians, Bosnians, Serbs, Armenians, Turks and
Greeks to the capital.

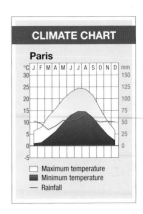

CLIMATE CHART

Paris

Maximum temperature
Minimum temperature
Rainfall

Dining on place des Vosges

Below: synagogue in the Marais
Bottom: traditional wine-seller

If Paris as a whole displays tolerance of other races and religions, 'immigration' is still used as a code word – particularly by right-wing extremists such as Jean-Marie Le Pen – to express their fear of foreigners. Ironically, the game of football has made a significant contribution to the advancement of race relations in France. In World and European Cups, which they won in 1998 and 2000 respectively, the French squad stood out as the most ethnically mixed in the world. Players come from Africa, the Caribbean and the Pacific Islands, all areas where France still has territories or strong links to its past as a colonial power. The team's hero in the 1998 World Cup, Zinédine Zidane, was a French-born North African. After France's victory, he appeared on the cover of a conservative national magazine draped in the French flag, and the Arc de Triomphe was draped with his face. Despite the team's disappointing performance in the 2002 competition, Zidane remains a national hero.

RELIGION

The majority of people in Paris are nominally Roman Catholic. However, France has the largest Muslim population in Europe, and Europe's largest Jewish community outside Russia, of which around 200,000 live in Paris. The city is home to only a few Protestants, and Eastern Orthodox believers are a vanishing minority.

ECONOMY

The Ile de France is the largest industrial centre in France, contributing 30 percent of the country's gross domestic product. Main industries in the region include printing and publishing, aerospace, electronics, automobiles and pharmaceuticals. There is very little manufacturing industry in Paris itself, however, due to high rents and lack of space. The service sector is the main employer here, with banks, insurance companies, company headquarters and public administration offices. The city is the financial centre of the country, with the Paris

Stock Exchange the fifth most active in the world. Paris is also France's largest consumer market and the focal point of all communications systems. Income from tourism is steadily increasing.

ADMINISTRATION

After the French Revolution of 1789 France was divided up for the first time into 89 *départements* plus the Territoire de Belfort in the east (which had the status of a *département*). Changes were continually made in the years that followed, more of interest to administrators than to travellers. After the last regional reform, France was divided up into 22 regions with 95 *départements*.

The area of Paris located within its famously busy ring road, the *périphérique,* is divided into 20 *arrondissements* (municipal districts); each *arrondissement* is run by its own *maire* (mayor) and is divided into four *quartiers* (quarters). The *arrondissements* are numbered and run outwards in a snail-shaped pattern from the Ile de France, the island on which Notre-Dame is located (No 1), to the northeast (No 20). When Parisians communicate where they live, whether to the tax office or at a party, they quote the number of their *arrondissement*. On letters, the number appears at the end of the postcode (ie. 75008 signifies the eighth *arrondissement*).

> **Orientation**
> House numbers always start at the part of a street nearest the Seine. In streets parallel to the river the house numbers usually run from east to west.

Marilyn Monroe at Fnac

HISTORICAL HIGHLIGHTS

3rd century BC The Celtic tribe of the Parisii settles on the Ile de la Cité, founding the settlement of Lucotesia.

58–52 BC Caesar conquers Gaul. The Celts set fire to their settlement and abandon it. A Roman colonial town is built on the same site: Lutetia.

c AD 250 Saint-Denis founds the first Christian community and is subsequently martyred.

3rd century Germanic tribes cross the Rhine and enter Gaul. Gallo-Roman towns build defensive fortifications.

451 Attila crosses the Danube and Rhine and heads towards Paris. A nun, Sainte-Geneviève, urges the people to resist and the town is left intact.

486 The Merovingian Clovis (c 466–511) defeats the army of the last Roman governor near Soissons. In 508 Paris becomes the capital of the Frankish Empire.

751–888 Under the Carolingians, Paris loses much of its political importance, but the city's economic importance increases. On four occasions, Paris is plundered and destroyed by the Normans.

987 Hugh Capet, a Parisian count, is made king. The Capetian dynasty rule France until the revolution. In Paris the upkeep of law and order is entrusted to a provost appointed by the king. The swamp to the north is drained, and settlements built on the right bank.

1108–54 Paris becomes a main trading centre under Louis VI, who campaigns against the unruly nobility of the Ile de France. With his adviser Suger, abbot of Saint-Denis, he re-establishes authority over the royal demesne. His support for schools paves the way for the city's role as capital of science and culture.

1226–70 Under Louis IX many of the injustices that had developed under the provosts are removed, and several schools of religious learning are founded in monasteries on the Seine's left bank.

1420 Paris surrenders to the English without a struggle. Nine years later, troops led by Joan of Arc try to retake the city, but without success. Paris is only finally recaptured in 1436.

1572 Under the regency of Catherine de Médicis, the Wars of Religion reach their climax in the Massacre of St Bartholomew's Day (23/24 August), when between 2,000 and 3,000 Protestant Huguenots in Paris are killed by Catholics.

1574–89 The dissolute lifestyle of Henry III incurs the wrath of the Parisians. In 1588 the citizens rebel, and the king flees. His death marks the end of the House of Valois.

1589–1610 Unable to take Paris after a five-year siege, Henry IV of Bourbon-Navarre converts to Catholicism. After the long siege the city recovers and the economy flourishes.

1610–43 Under Louis XIII, France's *Grand Siècle* (Great Century) begins. Cardinal Richelieu, a minister from 1624, attempts to unify all political power under the king.

1643–1715 Civil disturbances force Louis XIV to flee in 1648 to St-

Germain-en-Laye. From 1668 he has his father's hunting-lodge at Versailles extended; in 1682 he shifts the seat of government to his new palace there.

1789 The Estates-General are called to Versailles. The Third Estate demands that powers be verified in common. Louis XVI refuses. Troop concentrations result in the citizens of Paris storming the Bastille on 14 July.

1792–3 On 13 August 1792 the King is arrested, and France declared a republic on 21 September 1792. The King is guillotined on 21 January 1793.

1799–1814 The first Directory (1795) is followed by the Consulate, with Napoleon as First Consul. On 18 May 1804 he is proclaimed emperor

1815 After the fall of Napoleon, the Bourbons return to power with the accession of Louis XVIII.

1830–48 After the July Revolution of 1830, Louis-Philippe d'Orléans ascends the French throne. He is deposed in the February Revolution of 1848 and the Second Republic is declared. Louis Napoleon, a nephew of Napoleon I, becomes its president.

1852–70 After a *coup d'état*, Louis Napoleon proclaims the Second Empire on 2 December 1852.

1870–71 The Third Republic is declared on 4 September 1870. Paris capitulates to Prussian siege on 28 January 1871. A rebellion led by a workers' council, the Paris Commune, is bloodily suppressed after several fierce street battles (22–28 May 1871).

1871–1914 Paris prospers. International exhibitions of 1878, 1889 and 1900 draw attention to Paris.

1914–18 During World War I the city is spared from capture thanks to the Battle of the Marne (1914).

1940–4 On 14 June 1940 Paris is captured by German troops without a shot being fired. The Resistance, directed from London by de Gaulle, becomes increasingly active in Paris, especially in 1944. On 26 August, de Gaulle and the Allies enter the liberated city.

1946 The Fourth Republic.

1958 After a military coup in Algiers (13 May), the Fifth Republic is declared, with General de Gaulle as its president (until 1969).

1968 In May Paris is rocked by an uprising which swells from student unrest in the Latin Quarter to a nation-wide outbreak of strikes.

1969 Les Halles, the old food market in the centre of Paris, is shifted to Rungis near Orly Airport.

1981 The Socialist François Mitterrand becomes president and initiates a plan to rejuvenate Paris.

1989 Bicentenary of the Revolution.

1995 Jacques Chirac elected president.

1998 France hosts and wins the football World Cup.

2001 Socialist Bertrand Delanoë is elected Mayor of Paris. During the summers of 2002 and 2003 he turns the quays of the Seine into beaches.

2002 France adopts the euro. Chirac re-elected as president after a close initial challenge from the Front National.

2003 France opposes war in Iraq.

Map opposite

1: The Islands

In the 3rd century BC, the Celtic tribe of the Parisii built their first huts on the Ile de la Cité, the largest island in the Seine. In 52BC, Roman legions conquered the settlement and founded *Lutetia Parisiorum* on the left bank. During the Middle Ages, the island was the centre of political, religious and judicial power, not only for Paris but for the whole of France. Nowadays, the island is the geographical centre of the capital and home to several of the city's main official buildings – the Conciergerie, the law courts, the police headquarters and the Hôtel-Dieu hospital. The churches of Sainte-Chapelle and the gothic behemoth Notre-Dame make the island the focal point for religious tourism in the city.

Stained-glass windows, Sainte-Chapelle

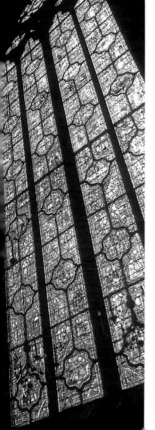

ACROSS PONT NEUF

This route starts at **Pont Neuf ❶** *(see box, right)*, the oldest bridge in Paris, despite its name. As you cross the river, look out for a flight of stairs behind the impressive equestrian statue of Henri IV, which stands on a small square platform between the two arms of the bridge – the statue, made in 1818, is a copy of an earlier one that had stood on this site since 1635 but was destroyed during the Revolution. The stairs lead to **square du Vert-Galant ❷**. Located at the tip of the Ile de la Cité, the leafy square has splendid views of the Louvre. The **Vedettes du Pont Neuf** riverboats depart from here every 30 minutes (10am–noon and 1.30–6.30pm in winter, also 9–10.30pm in summer, tel: 01 46 33 98 38).

From square du Vert-Galant, it is easy to access **place Dauphine ❸**, one of the loveliest and most elegant squares in Paris. Created in 1607 by Henri IV to offer a market for traders near the Palais de la Cité, the tranquil square is home to 32 white-stone town houses built around an enclosed triangular courtyard. Famous past residents include singer Yves Montand and his partner actress Simone Signoret. There are several attractive cafés, restaurants, art galleries and bookshops here, making it a pleasant place for a stroll or a leisurely breakfast.

Palais de la Cité

At the heart of the Ile de la Cité is the Palais de la Cité, the name for the complex of buildings that includes the Conciergerie and Gothic Sainte-Chapelle (both open daily Apr–Sept, 9.30am–6.30pm; Oct–Mar 10am–5pm, tel: 01 53 73 78 50) and the Palais de Justice (daily except Sun 1.30–6pm, tel: 01 44 32 50 00, www.ca-paris.justice.fr), headquarters of the French supreme court.

SAINTE-CHAPELLE

First stop at the Palais de la Cité is ★★★ **Sainte-Chapelle** ❹, the palace chapel and a masterpiece of soaring Gothic architecture. Between 1245 and 1248 the devout Louis IX (later St-Louis) had the original palace chapel converted by architect Pierre de Montreuil into an elaborate shrine to house holy relics acquired from the emperor of Byzantium in 1239; these relics include the

Star Attraction
● Sainte-Chapelle

Pont Neuf
There are 37 bridges in the French capital, of which the oldest is the massive Pont Neuf (ironically, the name means 'New Bridge'), built for Henri IV in 1607. Pont Neuf connects the westernmost tip of the Ile de la Cité with the two banks. In 1985 the Bulgarian-American artist Javacheff Christo – who specialises in large-scale, temporary outdoor installations – thrust the bridge into the limelight by enveloping the entire structure in fabric for his work *The Pont Neuf Wrapped*.

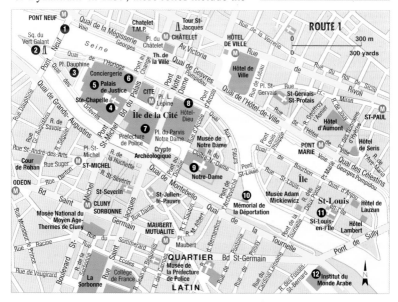

Map on page 19

so-called Crown of Thorns, believed to have been the one worn by Christ at his crucifixion. Such a treasure had to be closely guarded, and the king was the only person with a key to the reliquary chapel. Each Good Friday he would display its holy contents to the people in the Cour du Mai; for the rest of the year they were locked away.

During the French Revolution the reliquary shrine was melted down to make coins, the relics were moved – the Crown of Thorns is now in Notre-Dame – and the chapel was damaged. After the Revolution, restoration work on the chapel began in 1846.

THE EXTERIOR

The exterior of the building consists mainly of high tracery windows with pointed gable roofs and narrow flying buttresses between them. The chapel's height is 36m (120ft); its length is 17m (55ft). The façade of the western entrance, with its large Late Gothic rose window in flamboyant style, is flanked by two Late Gothic towers.

L'état, c'est moi

At the end of the Chambre Dorée is the courtroom of the first Civil Chamber, still in use today. Once the bedroom of King Louis IX, it was later used by the *parlement*. It was in this chamber that Louis XIV is reputed to have uttered the legendary phrase 'L'etat, c'est moi' ('I am the state'). The 12-member Revolutionary Tribunal sat in judgement here from 1793, sentencing some 2,700 people to death on the guillotine in 718 days.

LOWER AND UPPER CHAPELS

The ground-floor chapel, the **Chapelle Basse** (Lower Chapel), was used by the royal court for prayers. Low lines of columns separate the broad central nave from the noticeably narrow side aisles, and support the ribbed vault.

Most impressive, however, is Sainte-Chapelle's upper storey, or **Chapelle Haute** (Upper Chapel), reached via a spiral staircase from the Chapelle Basse. The beautiful, single-aisled chapel is a masterpiece of High Gothic architecture and was used exclusively by the royal family and the canons. The magnificent 13th-century stained glass, which depicts 1,134 scenes from the Bible in 85 major panels, is without equal anywhere in Paris. Sainte-Chapelle is unique among Gothic buildings for its medieval frescoes, which have all been restored. The delicately arcaded apse used to form part of the reliquary altar, and there was once an organ on the western wall.

Carved-and-gilded decoration, Sainte-Chapelle

PALAIS DE JUSTICE

The ★★ **Palais de Justice ❺**, or Palace of Justice, can also be reached via the Cour de Mai. During the French Revolution, the gate leading to the dungeons was situated to the right of the steps, and it was from here that the condemned were driven in carts to their death on the place de la Concorde.

A flight of steps leads up to the front of the building; inside is the **Galerie Marchande** (Merchants' Gallery). Until the revolution this was one of the busiest places in Paris – a meeting spot for lawyers, judges and clients. To the right is the **Salle des Pas Perdus** (Hall of Lost Steps), the former **Grande Chambre** (Large Chamber) and the old palace hall, known as the **Chambre Dorée** (Gilded Chamber) owing to its lavish decoration (1509). After a fire in 1618 the gallery was rebuilt by Salomon de Brosse as a two-aisled basilica; it assumed its present-day appearance after it burnt down a second time due to the insurrectionary Communards (1871).

On the left, just before the Salle des Pas Perdus, is the **Galerie des Prisonniers**. **Galerie Saint-Louis**, completed in 1877, then leads off to **Galerie Lamoignon**. At the end of this gallery is the **Vestibule de Harlay**, adorned with statues of statesmen including Louis IX and Napoleon I. The **Galerie de la Première Présidence** with the Cour d'Appel (Court of Appeal) leads to the exit.

Star Attraction
● **Palais de Justice**

Below: Palais de Justice
Bottom: Tricolore

Map on page 19

Notable inmates
Marie-Antoinette, the wife of Louis XVI, was not the only celebrity prisoner held at the Conciergerie during the Revolution. Other notable inmates included Louis's favourite mistress, Madame du Barry, Jean-Paul Marat's murderer Charlotte Corday and the poet André Chenier. Ironically, the Conciergerie was later a prison to Revolutionary leaders including Danton and Robespierre, and even the public prosecutor, Fouquier-Tinville.

THE CONCIERGERIE

At the corner of the Palais de Justice, on boulevard du Palais, is the first Parisian public clock, the **Tour d'Horloge**, built by the German horologer Heinrich von Vic in 1370. The clocktower marks the corner of the ★★ **Conciergerie ❻**. This imposing edifice was built as a Merovingian fortress but was used as a royal palace under the Capetians. In 1358, during the reign of Charles V, the Capetian royals moved to the Louvre and the old palace was entrusted to a royal caretaker *(concierge)* – hence the name. The Conciergerie rose to notoriety during the Revolution, when it held nearly 2,600 prisoners, including Marie-Antoinette. The writer Honoré de Balzac consequently dubbed the building the 'antechamber of scaffold'.

Adjacent to the Tour d'Horloge are three more towers: the **Tour de César**, **Tour d'Argent** and **Tour Bonbec**. Although the towers look medieval, they actually date from the mid-19th century. César, to the right of the entrance of the Conciergerie, was the home of Fouquier-Tinville, public prosecutor under the Terror of 1794.

GROUND FLOOR

The tour of the building begins at the Cour d'Entrée. The first room is the **Salle des Gardes** (guardroom), in use as early as the 14th century.

Bars in the Salle des Gens d'Armes

On rue de Paris, where up to 200 people awaited execution during the revolution, lies the **Salle des Gens d'Armes**, a huge Gothic hall – 70m (230ft) by 30m (100ft) – one of the mightiest secular structures of the Middle Ages. It was built during the reign of Philip IV (1285–1314), and served as a banqueting hall and recreation room for the royal household. The room was renovated in 2000, improving the light inside.

FIRST AND SECOND FLOORS

North of the hall, a spiral staircase and passageway lead to the palace kitchen, **Cuisine St-Louis**, built c 1353. Note the huge open fireplaces in each of the four corners – a different fireplace was used for each type of cooking (one for frying, one for baking, etc). This is where meals for the royal household, roughly 3,000-strong, were prepared.

At the end of rue de Paris is the section of the prison, reconstructed in 1989, that was used in the French Revolution. The lodges on either side of the entrance belonged to the guards and clerk. Further on, to the left, is the **Salle de la Toilette**, where prisoners were prepared for execution.

The upper storey contains the cells occupied by the more 'privileged' prisoners, as well as a room bearing the names of every single one of the 2,780 people executed during the French Revolution.

THE CHAPELLE DES GIRONDINS

After a small exhibition documenting the history of the building is a stairway leading down to the **Chapelle des Girondins**. It was in this chapel that the moderate Girondins who supported Danton spent their last hours. Marie-Antoinette was imprisoned here from 11 September 1793 until her execution on 16 October of the same year, in a small cell that used to be behind the altar.

The starting-point of the tour is reached once more by crossing the **Cour des Femmes**, where women were allowed to exercise; a reconstruction of Marie-Antoinette's cell is on the left.

Below: Jean-Paul Marat's murderer, Charlotte Corday, was imprisoned in the Conciergeirie
Bottom: Conciergerie towers

Map on page 19

Island markets

On quai aux Fleurs, a flower market – the Marché aux Fleurs – takes place daily except Sunday beneath the imposing façades of the administrative buildings on place Louis-Lépine. On Sunday mornings a bird market, the Marché aux Oiseaux, is held here instead. There are fine views of the Ile Saint-Louis to the east and the Hôtel de Ville (town hall, *see page 78*) to the north from here.

Marché aux Oiseaux

The Quays

East of the boulevard du Palais are the Parisian police headquarters, the **Préfecture de Police ❼**; this is also the headquarters of Interpol. Crime fans will be familiar with another corner of the Ile de la Cité – the **quai des Orfèvres**, immortalised in Simenon's *Maigret* detective stories.

Adjacent to place Louis-Lépine is the vast complex of buildings that make up the **Hôtel-Dieu ❽** (closed to visitors), a hospital built from 1866–78 on the site of a 7th-century convent.

Notre-Dame

The eastern end of the island is dominated by the Early Gothic Notre-Dame cathedral. **Place du Parvis de Notre-Dame**, the square in front of the cathedral, is generally considered to be the heart of Paris, and it is from here that all distances to other cities across France are measured. Excavations have revealed traces of Gallo-Roman and Early Medieval Paris, including the 6th-century Merovingian cathedral of St-Etienne. Finds are displayed in the **Crypte Archéologique** (daily 10am–5.30pm in summer, 10am–4.30pm in winter).

On the eastern side of the square is the cathedral itself: **★★★ Notre-Dame ❾** (open Mon–Fri 8am–6.45pm, Sat and Sun till 7.45pm; visits restricted during services). This huge behemoth dominates the city and remains its spiritual and architectural centrepiece. Construction work on the cathedral began in 1163 and was finished *c*1240, but extensions continued over the next 80 years. The scale of Notre-Dame exceeded all earlier churches – Paris became the capital only a few years before the foundation stone was laid, and the building was designed to reflect the power of the state and its church.

Western Façade

The lower storey of the cathedral, with its clean-lined smooth walls and solid pillars, is reminiscent of the Romanesque style. Above it is the King's Gallery (*c*1220). The storey with the rose window was probably inspired by the one at Laon cathedral in Picardy. The towers above (open 10am–4.30pm) are connected by a terrace closed by a balustrade; superb views of the city can be had from here.

Just as Gothic cathedrals were considered symbols of paradise, so the entrance façade, with its series of sculptures, was considered to be the gateway to heaven. The original cycle of figures over the entrance of Notre-Dame was partially damaged during the Revolution (the fragments are on display in the Musée de Cluny, *see page 60*), but numerous sculptures from St Mary's portal on the far left date from 1220–40. The figures on the section of doorway restored in the 19th century (surrounding the statue of the Virgin) include two saints closely associated with Paris: St-Denis, and Ste-Geneviève. The Judgement Portal in the middle shows Christ at the Last Judgement, with sculptures of angels and the kneeling figures of Mary Magdalene and John the Baptist. The two rows of figures on the door lintel below also portray the Last Judgement; the figures of Christ and the Apostles are 19th-century reconstructions.

On the right is St Anne's Portal. The figures on the lintel and tympanum (1150–65) were probably constructed for the building that formerly stood on the site, the cathedral of St-Etienne. Along with a few remains found in 1977, they are the oldest masterpieces of Gothic art in Paris.

Star Attraction
● Notre-Dame

Below: the rose window
Bottom: western façade

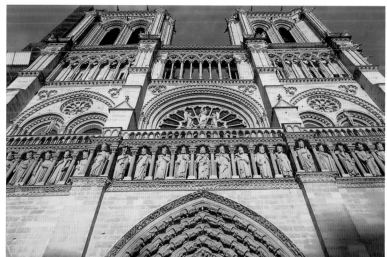

Map on page 19

The cathedral's gargoyles, which resemble mythical creatures, are the work of Eugène Viollet-le-Duc, who restored the cathedral in the 19th century.

NORTHERN AND SOUTHERN TRANSEPTS

Like Sainte-Chapelle *(see pages 19–20)*, constructed shortly before it, the façade of Notre-Dame's north transept, built during the mid-13th century, represents the second Parisian Gothic style. The portal and the two fake portals on either side of the façade are crowned by pointed triangles of stone, with fine finials between them. On the portal pillar is a statue of the Virgin; this is the only original work preserved here. On the south transept the portal is consecrated to St-Etienne, patron saint of the Merovingian structure that formerly stood on the site. Sculptured figures on the portal recount his life and martyrdom. The statues of the Apostles and of St-Etienne are copies of the originals, which were damaged.

THE INTERIOR

The mighty interior of the five-naved Notre-Dame always seems to be shrouded in a mystical half-light. The side-aisles, which are broken up by the transepts that are hardly any higher than the nave, continue on into the choir as double ambulatories.

Notre-Dame and Victor Hugo

The cathedral began to decay in the 17th century, but restoration by 19th-century Gothic revivalist Viollet-le-Duc began in 1814, partly as a result of interest in the building stirred by Victor Hugo's celebrated novel *Notre-Dame de Paris (The Hunchback of Notre-Dame)*. The novel, a weighty, multi-layered tome, first published in 1831, has since been adapted for film (including a Disney animation) and theatre. It follows the plight of the hunchback bellringer, Quasimodo, who strives to protect his gipsy love, Esmerelda.

Anthony Quinn as Quasimodo in the film The Hunchback of Notre-Dame

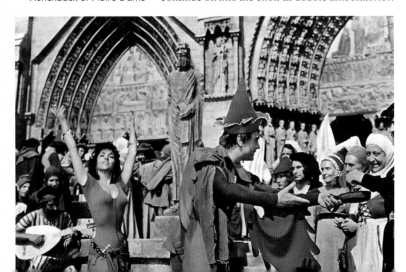

Additional chapels are attached to the outer side-aisles. The interior elevation of the centre aisle wall (reconstructed in the area of the crossing by Viollet-le-Duc in the 19th century) was formerly four storeys high and is Early Gothic, as are the sturdy round columns of the arcade and the sexpartite ribbed vault above the centre aisle; this was replaced in the High Gothic period by an oblong rib vault over one bay, and continuing wall shafts down to the base of the piers.

The interior of the cathedral was ransacked during the Revolution, and the choir stalls and a few memorial slabs are all that now remain of its medieval furnishings. A Gothic statue of the Virgin, on the southeastern pillar of the crossing, is said to work miracles. The Gothic high altar fell victim to Baroque modernisation in the reign of Louis XIV.

THE WINDOWS

In the 18th century the cathedral's windows were enlarged, but the interior was still very gloomy, so in 1756 the medieval stained glass was replaced by brighter panes. The original colours were only retained in the rose windows. The western rose window (c1230) shows the Virgin at its centre. Surrounding her are kings, virtues and vices, months of the year and signs of the zodiac. The Virgin is also at the centre of the northern rose window (c1250), this time in the company of figures and scenes from the Old Testament. The southern rose window (c1270) shows Christ surrounded by apostles and martyrs.

MEMORIAL DE LA DEPORTATION

At the eastern tip of the island, on square de l'Ile de France, is the **Mémorial de la Déportation ❿**. Designed by G.H. Pingusson and erected in 1962, the monument stands as a reminder of the 200,000 French who died in concentration camps during World War II. A pitch-black staircase leads down to a crypt (daily 10am–noon and 2–5pm), where the names of deportees are inscribed on the walls.

Mémorial de la Déportation

Map on page 19

ILE ST-LOUIS

The quiet quays of this little island in the Seine can be reached via the pedestrian footbridge of Pont St-Louis. It is certainly worth taking a stroll along the narrow streets here, past the elegant façades with their quiet inner courtyards behind (note that most of these mansions are private, so you'll only be able to admire the outside). One place to stop on your walk around the island is Glacier Berthillon (31 rue St-Louis-en-l'Ile), an ice-cream parlour and Parisian institution, where dozens of ice-cream flavours are available (note that, strangely, Berthillon is closed during the summer months).

Below: overlooking the Seine
Bottom: St-Louis-en-l'Ile

PRIVATE MANSIONS

The Ile St-Louis originally consisted of two mud-banks owned by the cathedral chapter that were handed over by royal command in 1614. After the channel dividing them had been filled in, the resulting island then had its circumference dyked and connection to the shore established via two bridges. From 1618 craftsmen began to settle on the Ile St-Louis, and in 1638 the island became a popular building site for rich nobles, who erected their *hôtels particuliers* (private mansions) here to escape the unhealthy confines of the city centre. One such building to the east of the island is the rococo-fronted Hôtel Chenizot at 51 rue St-Louis-en-l'Ile.

On the same road, at No 2, is the **Hôtel de Lambert,** designed by Le Vau (advisor to Louis XIV and one of the architects of Versailles) and constructed between 1640 and 1652 for Lambert de Thorigny, president of the parliament at that time. This is probably the most important mansion on the island, though its simple exterior gives no indication of the sheer wealth of decoration within. The writer and philosopher Voltaire (1694–1778) is believed to have lived here at some point, and the building was a popular meeting place for artists during the 19th century.

Located on the quai d'Anjou is the **★ Hôtel Lauzun,** its Louis XIV interior decoration still

almost entirely intact. As with other *hôtels par-ticuliers* situated along the quays of the Ile St-Louis, the layout of this mansion and its grounds is the reverse of the usual Paris ground-plan (the *Corps de Logis* is on the Seine side, with the court-yard and outbuildings behind it). Le Vau was also responsible for this palace, which at one time belonged to the Richelieu family. In the mid-19th century, the eccentric pair Charles Baudelaire and Théophile Gautier also lived here. The house (open Apr–Oct, weekend afternoons) has been the property of the city since 1928.

Plaques on several of the houses bear the names of the famous people who once lived on the island. Many of them were magistrates and financiers, whose names are long forgotten; one more familiar resident was the poet André Breton (1896–1966).

ST-LOUIS-EN-L'ILE

On rue St-Louis-en-l'Ile is the church of **St-Louis-en-l'Ile ⓫**, built in 1664 and originally de-signed by Le Vau. The church was not completed until 1725, however, long after the architect's death in 1670. The side tower was added later, in 1765. The interior, designed according to a cruciform ground-plan, consists of a barrel-vaulted nave and accompanying side-aisles.

Star Attraction
● Institut du Monde Arabe

Institut du Monde Arabe
An option to finish this route is to cross over the Pont de Sully at the eastern tip of the Ile St-Louis to reach the ★★ **Institut du Monde Arabe** (IMA) ⓬ (1 rue des Fossés-St-Bernard, 5th, open daily except Mon 10am–6pm). Designed to showcase and promote the art and culture of the Arab world, the institute was designed by Jean Nouvel and opened in 1987. A museum covers the development of Arabic-Islamic art and civilisation in permanent and temporary exhibi-tions. Some 240 photoelectric cells were intended to control the light within the building but the system never worked. The institute has a library and several attractive cafés.

Institut du Monde Arabe

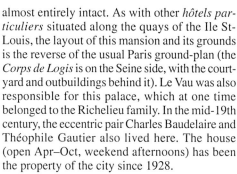

Maps below and on page 36

2: The Louvre

Over the centuries, the ★★★**Louvre** ⑬ has functioned as a fortress, prison, palace, administration centre and world-class museum and art gallery. Vast reorganisation and expansion since the 1980s – a result of the late François Mitterrand's *grands projets* scheme *(see page 91)* – doubled the gallery space to more than 6 hectares (15 acres), ensuring the Louvre's status as the largest museum in the world. You can easily while away half a day here, much longer if your schedule and stamina allow.

THE BUILDING

In 1984 foundations discovered beneath the Cour Carrée proved that a crusader castle once existed on this site. Built as a bulwark beside the Seine during the reign of Philippe Auguste (1180–1223), it housed the state treasure, the city archives and an armoury. Charles V had the city walls extended in 1370, and the Louvre then lost its military importance. The king had windows built into the fortress, housed his library in one of the towers and, during the last

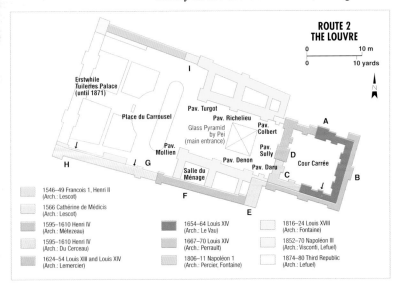

**ROUTE 2
THE LOUVRE**

0 — 10 m
0 — 10 yards

N

Erstwhile Tuileries Palace (until 1871)

Place du Carrousel

Pav. Turgot

Pav. Richelieu

Glass Pyramid by Pei (main entrance)

Pav. Colbert

A

Pav. Mollien

Pav. Sully

D

Pav. Denon

Cour Carrée

H

G

Salle du Ménage

Pav. Daru

C

B

F

E

1546–49 Francois 1, Henri II (Arch.: Lescot)

1566 Cathérine de Médicis (Arch.: Lescot)

1595–1610 Henri IV (Arch.: Métezeau)

1595–1610 Henri IV (Arch.: Du Cerceau)

1624–54 Louis XIII and Louis XIV (Arch.: Lemercier)

1654–64 Louis XIV (Arch.: Le Vau)

1667–70 Louis XIV (Arch.: Perrault)

1806–11 Napoléon 1 (Arch.: Percier, Fontaine)

1816–24 Louis XVIII (Arch.: Fontaine)

1852–70 Napoléon III (Arch.: Visconti, Lefuel)

1874–80 Third Republic (Arch.: Lefuel)

years of his regency (until 1380), he turned the Louvre into a magnificent residence.

FRANÇOIS I TO HENRI IV

During the Hundred Years' War (1340–1453) the Louvre stood empty. However, in the reign of François I the royals returned, and work began on redesigning the building in the Italian Renaissance style under the architect Pierre Lescot (1510–78). Lescot's façade [**C**] is considered to be one of the finest works of the French Renaissance. François's successors Henri's II, III and IV further extended this part of the building.

After the death of Henri II, his widow Cathérine de Médicis (1564–72) commissioned the construction of a palace, the Palais des Tuileries, 500m (1,640ft) west of the Louvre, on the site of a former tilery (hence the name). As part of a plan to join the Louvre and the Palais des Tuileries, Cathérine commissioned the Petite Galerie [**E**]. Under Henri IV the Grande Galerie, or Galerie du Bord de l'Eau [**F**], was built along the Seine; this long, two-storey construction had arcades on the courtyard side and a closed ground-floor façade looking on to the Seine. The façade along its eastern section as far as the Pont du Carrousel is the only part of the original structure remaining. The initials H and G on the façade are those of Henri IV and his favourite mistress Gabrielle d'Estrées.

LOUIS XIII AND LOUIS XIV

From 1624–54, under Louis XIII and then Louis XIV, the Palais de l'Horloge [**D**], which dominates the centre of the west front, was built. In 1661 Louis XIV rejected a design by Bernini for the east front of the Louvre [**B**], choosing instead a neoclassical colonnade by Parisian doctor Claude Perrault. In 1673 construction work began, but there were insufficient funds to complete the project, mainly due to the decision to build Versailles. After the royal court had moved to the latter, the Louvre remained incomplete. The

Star Attraction
● **The Louvre**

Below: Louvre courtyard
Bottom: Louis XIV

Maps
on pages
30 & 36

Smiler

The enigmatic smile of Leonardo's much-revered *Mona Lisa* (*La Joconde* in French) was unfavourably described by the 20th-century novelist, poet, dramatist and travel writer Lawrence Durrell as that 'of a woman who has just dined off her husband'.

Louvre arcades

east and north wings were unroofed, and the colonnade was only completed in 1755. After the king had moved out, the newly founded academies were transferred to the former palace.

THE REVOLUTION AND NAPOLEON I

During the Revolution, it was decided to turn the former royal palace into a museum, ironically fulfilling the plans of Louis XVI, the king just beheaded at the guillotine. Opened in 1793 the museum, the Musée Central des Arts, benefited from the growing collection of national treasures, augmented by Napoleon's efforts to relocate much of Europe's artistic wealth following his victorious campaigns in Italy, Austria and Germany. During Napoleon's reign (1806–11), his court architects Percier and Fontaine added a third storey to the wings around the Cour Carrée and completed the connection to the Palais des Tuileries, where he himself lived. After Napoleon's defeat at Waterloo in 1815, many of the stolen masterpieces were reclaimed by their rightful owners.

LOUIS XVIII TO THE THIRD REPUBLIC

With Louis XVIII reinstated as King (1816–24), the architect Fontaine worked on the Pavillon de Rohan. Here, **[I]** a gateway opens out into the rue de Rivoli. In 1852 Napoleon III commissioned Visconti to erect two symmetrical sections between the Louvre and the gallery buildings. A library was housed in the north wing, while the south wing was dedicated to staterooms. The Palais des Tuileries was badly damaged by fire laid by the insurrectionists of the Commune in 1871, and in 1882 what remained of it was completely demolished except for two corner pavilions.

THE 20TH CENTURY

In 1981 President François Mitterrand began a vast renovation of the museum, calling it the *Projet du Grand Louvre*. In 1989, the bicentenary of the

French Revolution, the ★★★ **Louvre Pyramid** was inaugurated as the museum's new main entrance, in the Cour Napoléon. Designed by Sino-American architect I.M. Peï, the 19-m (62-ft) glass structure forms part of the city's 'royal axis' that runs from the Cour Carrée of the Louvre past the obelisk on place de la Concorde and the Arc de Triomphe up to the Grande Arche in La Défense, to the west of the city *(see page 46)*. Initially a hot potato, it is now considered one of the most successful of Mitterrand's legacies. A car park and a shopping arcade, with various fashion boutiques and shops devoted to interior design and novelties, are situated beneath the Cour du Carrousel.

Star Attractions
● **Louvre Pyramid**
● **Musée du Louvre**

THE COLLECTION

The ★★★ **Musée du Louvre** (open Thurs–Sun 9am–6pm, Mon and Wed 9am–9.45pm, closed Tues and public holidays; tickets are valid all day and allow re-entry into the museum) is divided into three wings (Richelieu in the north, Sully in the east and Denon in the south). The collections are spread over seven different sections, each assigned its own colour to facilitate orientation. The following is a selection of the highlights from the various different sections

A good place to start is the exhibition on the Medieval Louvre, en route to the Crypte Sully

Jacques-Louis David's Consecration of the Emperor Napoleon and the Coronation of the Empress Josephine

Maps
on pages
30 & 36

Beat the queues
There are several entrances to the Louvre, and the queues are often shorter if you enter via the Carrousel from rue de Rivoli or directly from Palais-Royal Métro, rather than through the Pyramid. If you have a museum pass or have bought a ticket in advance (available at the Virgin Megastore in the Carrousel shopping centre), you can queue-jump and use the additional entrance through the Porte des Lions. Note that the museum tends to be less busy on late-night opening on Wednesday.

under the Cour Carrée, where the remains of Philippe-Auguste's fort and keep, and some of the artefacts discovered in excavations in the 1980s, can be seen.

On the ground floor of the Sully and Richelieu wings are the **Oriental Antiquities**, which include the Mesopotamian prayer statuette of Ebih-il (around 2400 BC), with striking lapiz lazuli eyes, and the black basalt Babylonian Code of Hammurabi (1792–1750 BC), one of the world's first legal documents.

On the south side of the Sully Wing you will find the graceful Hellenic statue ★★★ *Venus de Milo* (2nd century BC), bought by the French government for 6,000FF in 1820 from the Greek island of Milos. From here, head to the Denon Wing to see the Etruscan ★ *Sarcophagus of the Reclining Couple*. Continuing along the ground floor level, you will reach the Italian sculpture section and Michelangelo's ★★★ *Slaves* (1513–1520), sculpted in marble for Pope Julius II's tomb but never finished, and Canova's neoclassical *Psyche Revived by the Kiss of Cupid* (1793).

In the Denon Wing, on the first floor, is the ★★★ *Mona Lisa* (1503) – *La Joconde* in French. The first incumbent in the Louvre, Leonardo da Vinci's small painting of a Florentine noblewoman rests securely behind glass since her knife assault in the 1980s. But don't ignore the many

Autumn by Poussin

other masterpieces hanging in this gallery, including more by Leonardo and works by Raphaël, Titian and Veronese, as well as Caravaggio's ★ *The Fortune Teller*.

On the same floor is the Grande Galerie, which starts at the top of the Escalier Daru opposite the ★★ *Winged Victory of Samothrace* (2nd century BC), the Hellenistic stone figurehead commemorating a victory at sea. Here hang large format French paintings of the 19th century, with Delacroix's ★★ *Liberty Leading the People*, Géricault's ★ *Raft of the Medusa* and David's ★ *Sabine Women*. The Spanish School, with masterpieces by El Greco and Goya, is nearby.

The second floor of the Richelieu and Sully wings are dedicated to paintings and include Rembrandt's ★★ *Bathsheba Bathing* (1654).

The beautifully renovated Richelieu Wing houses a vast collection of French sculpture on the ground floor and is focused around two splendid sculpture courts, home to Guillaume Coustou's two giant ★★ *Marly Horses*.

ADDITIONAL MUSEUMS

In a separate wing (107 entrance at rue de Rivoli) are three other collections. The **Musée des Arts Décoratifs** (open Tues, Thur, Fri 11am–6pm, Wed 11am–9pm, Sat–Sun 10am–6pm) presents a survey of interior design, from medieval tapestries to 21st-century design.

In the same wing, the **Musée des Arts de la Mode et du Textile** covers Paris fashions and textiles from the 16th century to the present day. Each year it mounts a large display focusing on a different aspect of its collection, from the earliest existing dresses to the ground-breaking designs of the big-name couturiers of the 20th century, such as Christian Dior and Yves Saint-Laurent.

Upstairs, the **Musée de la Publicité** (opening times as above) , designed by architect Jean Nouvel, is home to a rich collection of around 100,000 posters from the Middle Ages to the present day. Only a fraction of the vast collection can ever be exhibited at one time.

Star Attractions
● **International painting and sculpture from across the ages**

Below: Leonardo's Mona Lisa
Bottom: Bather *by Ingrès*

Map below

3: The Tuileries to La Défense

This route continues along the traditional royal axis that runs in a straight line west from the Louvre, through the Tuileries, along the Champs-Elysées, to the Arc de Triomphe. The addition of the Grande Arche at La Défense in 1989 further extended this axis. It would be exhausting to visit every site included in this route; instead, pick and choose sites of interest as you make your way west. You could also choose to walk this route in the afternoon, following a morning at the Louvre.

ARC DE TRIOMPHE DU CARROUSEL

This route starts on the east side of the Tuileries, at the ★**Arc de Triomphe du Carrousel ⑭**, which stands as a *point de vue* to the east of the Jardin des Tuileries. Work began on this monument and on its larger namesake, the Arc de Triomphe de l'Etoile, in 1806, with both arches intended to glorify the victorious campaigns of Napoleon. The Arc de Triomphe du Carrousel was designed by imperial architects La Fontaine and Percier, and was a neoclassical copy of the Roman triumphal arch for Septimius Severus and Constantine. With its three gateways (20m/65ft wide, 15m/50ft high), it forms the entrance to the

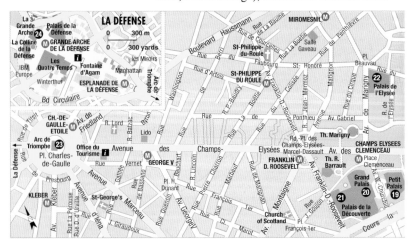

courtyard of the Tuileries and was consecrated in 1808. It was originally crowned by the four bronze horses from St Mark's in Venice (brought back to Paris as booty along with numerous other artistic treasures). The present four horses are the work of Bosio, and were placed there in 1828.

The view through the arch across place de la Concorde and all the way to the Arc de Triomphe de l'Etoile is superb, even though the arch looks somewhat forlorn, stuck in the middle of the large open space between the Louvre and the Jardin des Tuileries. (It was rather less isolated in front of the Palais des Tuileries, but the latter was pulled down in 1882.)

The area where the palace used to stand, between the Pavillon Marsan and the Pavillon de Flore, is now an open-air museum containing sculptures by Aristide Maillol, produced between 1900 and 1938.

THE TUILERIES

Between the Louvre and the place de la Concorde is the ★★ **Jardin des Tuileries** (Tuileries Gardens, open daily 7am–9pm in summer, 7.30am–7.30pm in winter), which Cathérine de Médicis originally laid out in front of her palace in Renaissance style after the death of her husband.

Star Attraction
● **Jardin des Tuileries**

Kids' stuff
The Tuileries Gardens are great for children. There's a new playing area for 3–7 year olds, designed by writers, painters and architects and including a maze. Other attractions include pony rides, trampolining and puppet-shows (théâtre de Guignol). Note that children aren't allowed to run on the grass. If you're looking for refreshment to keep the kids quiet, there are several restaurants in the park, including two open-air and two indoor ones.

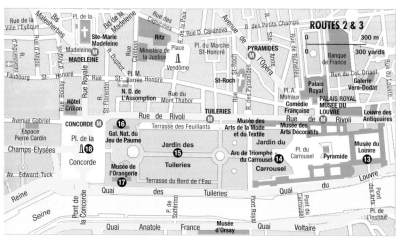

Map
on pages
36–7

*Below: sculpture by
Aristide Maillol
Bottom: benches in
the Tuileries*

In 1664 landscape architect André Le Nôtre was given the task of enlarging and redesigning the gardens. He laid out a parterre, and livened it up with two small pools and one large pool containing fountains, which formed the focal point of the geometrically designed park.

Statues were introduced to the gardens in the 18th century. From an artistic point of view the most valuable sculpture came from the then-dilapidated Château de Marly, although the sculptures around the large octagonal pond are also important; the pond sculptures are all the work of Coustou and Van Cleve, and show hermae representing the four seasons, recumbent river gods based on antique models and female allegories representing French rivers. New sculptures were added to commemorate the millennium in 2000.

RUE DE RIVOLI

On the north side of the Jardin des Tuileries is **rue de Rivoli**, its name a reminder of Napoleon's victory over the Austrians at Rivoli, north of Verona, in 1797. More than 500 houses were torn down in 1811, when construction work finally started on this street. The work was only completed in 1833, however – long after the emperor's abdication in 1814. The straight line of this street and the regimented design of the façades bordering it have been traditional in Paris since the time of Henri IV and Louis XVI. The arcaded passageways now contain shops aimed mainly at tourists.

The indoor riding arena of the Tuileries used to stand between rue de Castiglione and the place des Pyramides. The Constituent Assembly set up an assembly hall there in 1789, and the First Republic was declared there on 21 September 1792.

THE JEU DE PAUME AND ORANGERIE

Napoleon III had the **Jeu de Paume** ⓰ (open Tues noon–9.30pm, Wed–Fri noon–7pm, Sat, Sun 10am–7pm) built as an indoor court for real tennis, and also constructed a hothouse opposite it, known as the **Musée de l'Orangerie** ⓱ (closed until summer 2004 for restoration). The latter, although currently inaccessible, is home to Claude Monet's world-famous paintings of water-lilies, in which the great Impressionist painter captured the play of colour on the water-lily pond in his Japanese garden at Giverny at different times of day.

Star Attraction
● **place de la Concorde**

PLACE DE LA CORCORDE

After the Treaty of Aachen in 1748, which ended the Austrian War of Secession, Paris decided to honour King Louis XV with an equestrian statue. In 1755, construction work duly began on the imposing ★★ **place de la Concorde** ⓲, based on plans by the architect Gabriel. The royal square in which the statue of Louis XV and two fountains were erected took the form of a rectangle with the edges rounded off, surrounded by balustrades and water-free ditches. The top storeys of the two large buildings to the north of the square carry on the theme of the Louvre colonnade, and are closed off at the side by gabled corner pavilions. The monument to the king was erected in 1763, and the square was duly consecrated as place Louis XV on order of the city senate. In 1792 the square was renamed place de la Révolution, and the equestrian statue of the king was melted down to make copper coins.

During the Directory in 1795 the square received its present-day name: Concorde Square. In the reign

Heads rolled
On the northern side of the place de la Concorde, where today the Statue of the City of Brest stands, Louis XVI was executed on 21 January 1793. Later the guillotine was shifted to the entrance to the Tuileries. According to official estimates, 1,119 people were decapitated here including Charlotte Corday, the Girondist leader, Queen Marie-Antoinette, Prince Philippe, Madame Dubarry, André Chénier and Robespierre.

The Arc du Triomphe du Carrousel

Map
on pages
36–7

*Below: Concorde's
Egyptian obelisk
Bottom: gilded
Parisian salamander*

of King Louis-Philippe (1830–48) the Cologne architect Hittorf began redesigning it, and the work was finally completed in 1854.

Since 1836 the centre of the place de la Concorde has been dominated by the almost 23-m (75-ft) high obelisk from Luxor, presented to Louis-Philippe (1830–48) by the Ottoman governor of Egypt (Mehmed Ali) in 1831. This pink granite monolith, which is nearly 3,200 years old and weighs around 230 tons, formerly stood in front of the Temple of Luxor. Hieroglyphs proudly recount the deeds of Ramesses II. The two fountains (also designed by Hittorf) on the left and right of the obelisk are modelled after those of St Peter's Square in Rome. The horsebreakers by Coustou (1745) were originally destined for the nearby Château de Marly. In 1798 they were positioned at the start of the Champs-Elysées, near the entrance to the Jardins des Tuileries, as a counterpiece to the groups displaying Renommée, the goddess of fame, and the god Mercury on winged horses, both by Coysevox (1702).

Leading south from the place de la Concorde is the Pont de la Concorde, built in 1791, from where there are glorious views of the square. On the north side of the square are two magnificent palaces built in the 18th century by Gabriel: one is the deluxe Hôtel Crillon, the other is home to a government ministry.

CHAMPS-ELYSÉES

The place de la Concorde provides magnificent views of the ★★ **avenue des Champs-Elysées** (Elysian Fields) as far as the Arc de Triomphe. This splendid avenue is considered by many – not only the French – to be the finest in the world. It provides a grand scenario for parades and other national events. Millions stroll up and down this 2-km (1¼-mile) long boulevard every year.

This *grand cours* was laid out by landscape architect André Le Nôtre as an extension of the straight avenue that led from the Jardin des Tuileries through an area of swampland to the heights of Chaillot. In 1670 the road was opened as a promenade for coaches as far as the Rond-Point. The section further west remained neglected and uninhabited, though it was still used now and then for military exercises. It was only during the Second Empire that the Champs-Elysées was finally lined with buildings, and it soon became a fashionable promenade.

Since the end of World War II the Champs have lost their image as the meeting-place of *tout Paris*, though whenever large demonstrations and parades are held – including the large parades held on 14 July – it becomes the focal point not just of Paris but of all France.

Between the mid-1970s and the early 1990s, the eight-lane avenue became increasingly congested with traffic, and the atmosphere was rather more downmarket. The Champs were dominated by boutiques aimed at tourists, fast-food restaurants, over-priced cafés and ice-cream parlours and chain cinemas. However, in 1992 Jacques Chirac, then mayor of Paris, decided to take matters in hand, dedicating a large budget to solving traffic congestion here. Encouraged, smart restaurant owners and fashion moguls rekindled their interest in the area, and in 1999 a swish branch of Paris tea store Ladurée opened at No 75. Louis Vuitton then opened a large store at No 101, and perfumiers Séphora and autombile firm Renault followed. Numerous other stylish boutiques and restaurants have opened in the streets surrounding the avenue recently. At last, things are looking up.

Star Attraction
● **Champs-Elysées**

Jardins des Champs-Elysées
From the place de la Concorde to the Rond Point des Champs-Elysées are the Jardins des Champs-Elysées, designed by Hittorf. Amid the gardens are the cultural centre l'Espace Pierre Cardin, dedicated to promoting Parisian cultural life, several theatres and the Ambassadeurs restaurant. A little further west, close to avenue Gabriel, is the American Embassy and the gardens of the British Embassy. The gardens of the Palais de l'Elysée are also located here; these may be visited on 'open-house days' (Journées Portes Ouvertes).

Along the Champs-Elysées from the Arc de Triomphe

Map on pages 36–7

Below: the Grand Palais
Bottom: Métro sign

PETIT PALAIS

Between the place de la Concorde and the avenue Franklin D. Roosevelt are the Grand Palais and Petit Palais. These, along with the Pont Alexandre III, were built on the occasion of the 1900 Universal Exhibition in ornate Belle Epoque style.

The rococo-style ★★ **Petit Palais** ⓲ (closed until 2004 for restoration) is distinctive for its monumental entrance. The sculptures on either side represent *The Seine and Her Tributaries* (left) and *The Four Seasons* (right). Since 1902 the Petit Palais has housed the Municipal Art Collection. Among the most notable works in the collection of paintings here are *Portrait of a Woman* by Lucas Cranach and a self-portrait by Rembrandt, although these are currently inaccessible to visitors owing to the extensive restoration of the palace.

GRAND PALAIS

On the corner of the Champs-Elysées is a monument to statesman Georges Clémenceau (1841–1929). On the other side of avenue Winston Churchill is the ★★ **Grand Palais** ⓴. Its roof is currently under restoration but the palais remains open to the public. With its 5,000sq m (5,980sq yds) of space, it is an important exhibition centre and hosts not only several major art exhibitions but also the Paris Motor Show every spring.

It's strongly advisable to book in advance (tel: 08 92 68 46 or visit www.fnac.com or www.virgin.com for tickets because the queues here tend to be long. Visitors with advance tickets may visit from 10am–1pm daily; those without reservations may visit 1–8pm (till 10pm on Wed).

PALAIS DE LA DÉCOUVERTE

Situated next to the Grand Palais is the **Palais de la Découverte** ㉑ (open Tues–Sat, 9.30am–6pm, Sun and bank hols 10am–7pm, www.palais-decouverte.fr). The museum showcases elementary and contemporary science through interactive experiments with a commentary by exhibition curators. It covers astronomy (there's a planetarium), biology, chemistry, mathematics, physics and earth sciences. There is an electrostatics room, a room devoted to the Sun, a room on the evolution of the earth and living species, plus an acoustics room.

> 👁 **Musée Marmottan**
> West of the place du Trocadéro, next to the Jardin du Ranelagh, is the Musée Marmottan (2 rue Louis-Boilly, open Tues–Sun 10am–6pm, tel: 01 44 96 50 33, www.marmottan.com). The museum holds the collection of Louis Marmottan (1856–1932) and is made up of Impressionist masterpieces, including works by Monet, Renoir, Manet and Gauguin. There is also some exceptional furniture from the First Empire.

PALAIS DE L'ELYSEE

A detour from place Clémenceau down avenue de Marigny will take you to the **Palais de l'Elysée** ㉒ (rue du Faubourg St-Honoré), the official seat of the French president since 1873 (open to the public only on Journées du Patrimoine, *see page 78*). The palace has changed hands and purposes over the centuries: it was built in 1722 by Claude Mollet and acquired by Madame de Pompadour in 1753. Foreign ambassadors resided here in the reign of Louis XV, but it was turned into a public ballroom during the Revolution. In 1806 it was given to Napoleon's sister Caroline. After Waterloo, Napoleon signed his second abdication declaration here.

Charles de Gaulle

ARC DE TRIOMPHE

At the far end of the Champs-Elysées is the ★★ **Arc de Triomphe** ㉓. In 1806, after the Battle of the Three Emperors at Austerlitz, Napoleon ordered the construction of a triumphal arch to honour his glorious armies and commemorate his victories.

Map on pages 36–7

Below: the Arc de Triomphe
Bottom: detail, Rude sculpture

His chosen architect was Jean-François Chalgrin (1739–1811), who decided to move the triumphal arch planned for the place de la Bastille to the end of the Champs-Elysées. Construction work was slow, and when Napoleon married Marie-Louise in 1810, only the foundations of the arch had been laid. Work tailed off after the fall of Napoleon and the return of the Bourbons, but Louis-Philippe (1836) brought the work on the arch to completion.

The colossal statues on the main façades glorify the insurrection of 1792 and Napoleon's victories. The most notable of the reliefs on the arch is the *Departure of the Volunteers of 1792*, also known as *La Marseillaise*, by Burgundian sculptor François Rude. The upper section of the structure is taken up by a frieze, with statues portraying the departure and glorious return of the *Grande Armée*. On the ledge above, round bucklers bear the names of Napoleon's battles, and the inside of the arch shows the names of 558 generals. In 1840 Napoleon's remains were brought home through the Arc de Triomphe.

During the Second Empire, the place de l'Etoile and the streets radiating from it were redesigned by Haussmann and Hittorf. Haussmann, appointed prefect of the Seine in 1853 by Napoleon III, began the great task of improving Paris, building bridges , laying out parks and redesigning the city's boulevards.

In 1921 an unknown French soldier, symbolising the 1,390,000 who fell in World War I, was laid to rest beneath the arch. The *Tombeau du Soldat Inconnu* (Tomb of the Unknown Soldier) was the first memorial of its type in the world.

The platform above the arch can be reached via a lift, and it provides one of the finest views of Paris (open Tues–Sat 10am–10.30pm, Apr–Oct until 11pm). Note that the best time to visit is early morning or evening, when it is quietest.

CENTRE NATIONAL DE LA PHOTOGRAPHIE

Contemporary photography exhibitions are held in the Hôtel Salomon de Rothschild, home to the **Centre National de la Photographie** (open daily except Tues noon–7pm, www.cnp-photographie.com). The museum puts on thematic and monographic shows by photographers from across the globe, including British Sam Taylor-Wood, Thomas Ruff, Tracey Moffat and Mariko Mori.

MUSÉE NISSIM DE CAMANDO

The **Musée Nissim de Camando** (63 rue de Monceau, open Wed–Sun 10am–5pm, www.ucad.fr) is a reconstruction of a fine 18th-century home. Inside is the remarkable collection of furniture, rugs, porcelain, gold and silver and paintings bequeathed to the French state in 1935 by Count Moïse de Camondo in memory of his son, Nissim, who was killed in action in 1917.

MUSÉE JACQUEMART-ANDRÉ

At 158 boulevard Haussmann is the **Musée Jacquemart-André** (open daily 10am–6pm). The museum displays a collection of art and furniture that once belonged to collector Edouard André (son of a wealthy banking family) and his wife, erstwhile society portrait painter, Nélie Jacquemart. The large reception rooms mostly cover the 18th-century French School, including paintings by Jean-Marc Nattier and furniture by Joesph, while the library is a showcase for Flemish masterpieces.

Centre National de la Photographie, just off the Champs-Elysées

Map on pages 36–7

Upstairs is the Italian collection, notably some exceptional Renaissance paintings. The diminutive *St George and the Dragon* (*c*1439–40) by Paolo Uccello is particularly appealing.

LA DÉFENSE

Winter Garden
The Musée Jacquemart-André has a Jardin d'Hiver (Winter Garden), with lush vegetation and a grand double-revolution marble staircase. At the top of the staircase is a Tiepolo fresco; another one is displayed on the ceiling of the former dining room (now the restaurant).

La Défense

La Défense lies to the west of the city, beyond the Pont de Neuilly and the Seine. The complex that makes up this satellite city symbolises France's architectural breakthrough into the 21st century. *Défense* is the name of the bronze sculpture by Barrias that was erected on the square in 1883 to commemorate the defence of Paris against the Prussian army in 1870. Now a veritable open-air museum of contemporary art, the square is surrounded by equally cutting-edge architecture. Around 100,000 people work here, and over 30,000 live here. The area contains all modern conveniences and entertainment facilities, schools, sports grounds and also a park.

One of the most distinctive buildings at La Défense, the ★ **Centre National des Industries et Techniques** (CNIT) was converted into a hotel with a congress centre. The roof, which at 90,000 sq m (107,600 sq yd) is larger than the place de la Concorde, is supported by only three arches spanning 284m (930ft).

THE GRANDE ARCHE

To the west, rounding off the view along the Louvre–Arc de Triomphe–La Défense axis, is the ★★ **Grande Arche ㉔**, a monumental marble gate 110m (360ft) high and 106m (345ft) wide designed by the Danish architect Otto van Spreckelsen, (open Wed–Mon, 10am–7pm, last ride at 6pm). The Human Rights Foundation is one of the institutions housed beneath its roof. The dark glass towers of insurance companies jostle for attention with the colossal oil company buildings and hotels. The huge Quatre Temps department store lies at the heart of this designer city, which stares down proudly – but also somewhat enviously – at the lively old metropolis spread out beneath its feet.

4: Around the Eiffel Tower

No visit to Paris would be complete without a trip to the Eiffel Tower, symbol of the city and of France herself. The metal giant looms over the area southwest of the centre. Adjacent are the Invalides, a complex of important military buildings, and, just east of there, one of the capital's most exceptional museums dedicated to the work of a single artist: the Musée Rodin. It's a good idea to walk this route in the morning, as the queues at the Eiffel Tower tend to be shortest early in the day.

Map below

Star Attractions
● Grande Arche de la Défense
● Eiffel Tower

EIFFEL'S TOWER

The 300-m (985-ft) high ★★★ **Tour Eiffel** ㉕ (Eiffel Tower, open daily 9.30am–11pm, till midnight mid-Jun–Aug, www.tour-eiffel.fr) was built according to plans by architect Gustave Eiffel between 28 January 1887 and 31 March 1889 for the Paris Universal Exhibition of 1889. 'Paris

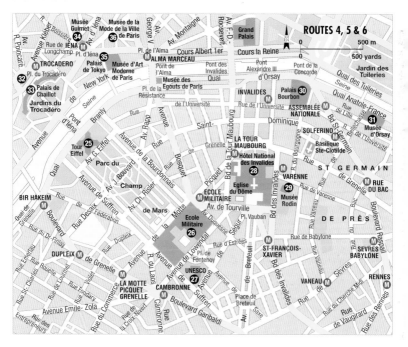

Map on page 47

Vital statistics

The tower weighs 7,000 tons, and consists of around 12,000 individual steel sections. A hefty 52 tons of paint are needed to give it just one coat. Despite its massive dimensions, the weight of the Eiffel Tower is distributed in such a way that each square centimetre of ground area is only subjected to 4kg (8.8lbs) of pressure (roughly equivalent to the weight of an average person sitting on a chair). Even during the fiercest storms, the top of the tower never moves more than 12cm (4¾in).

will be the only country with a 300-m flagpole,' he proudly declared. Initially, the reception to the tower was frosty, with the Opéra architect Charles Garnier and the novelist Guy de Maupassant among its most vocal opponents; Maupassant organised a protest picnic under the tower's legs – 'the only place out of sight of the wretched construction'.

Yet public support grew, and in 1916 the tower was granted a practical purpose: the first transoceanic radio contact was made from here in that year; radio programmes have been broadcast from the tower ever since. The 21-m (68-ft) high television antenna was erected in 1957. The uppermost platform contains a meteorological station as well as electronic equipment used for air traffic control.

The first platform, where there is a restaurant, is 57m (187ft) up, while the second platform (also with a restaurant) is at 115m (377ft). From the second platform, a lift takes visitors up to the third one, 300m (984ft) up, from which you can see for around 40 miles (65 km) on a clear day. There is a total of 1,652 steps. A tip is to take the stairs to the first floor and take the lift from there.

CHAMP DE MARS

The Eiffel Tower

Between the Eiffel Tower and the Ecole Militaire is the **Champ de Mars**, a field used under the

ancien régime for military exercises. In the 18th century it was the scene of early experiments in aviation, and the French physicist Jacques Alexandres César Charles made the first ascent in a hydrogen balloon here in 1783.

Star Attraction
● Ecole Militaire

ECOLE MILITAIRE

Beyond, on avenue de la Motte Piquet, is the ★★**Ecole Militaire** ㉖ (Military Academy). Madame de Pompadour, the mistress of Louis XV, had the idea of constructing an architectural monument in honour of the king, and the architect Jacques-Ange Gabriel was entrusted with the project. His design was modelled on the Hôtel des Invalides, but money was scarce and the building slow to complete. In 1773 the main part of the structure was ready; the courtyard of honour was finished one year later. Further additions were made in 1782, 1856 and 1865. However, the costly military school was short-lived – it only lasted until 1787, and its most famous pupil was Napoleon Bonaparte. Today, alongside the military academy, the building houses several other academic institutions.

The south of the building, with its colossal portico and dome, faces the Champ de Mars. The main façade, with its Cour d'Honneur enclosed by colonnades, borders avenue de Lowendal. The interior, which may only be visited by written permission of the military authorities (1 place Joffre) and then only as part of a conducted tour, contains almost entirely original decoration.

Below: Ecole Militaire
Bottom: Maison de l'UNESCO

UNESCO

On the south side of place de Fontenoy is the **Maison de l'UNESCO** ㉗ (open Mon–Fri 9am–12.30pm and 2.30–6pm). A combined achievement of the member states, the building was designed in a Y-shape by Marcel Breuer (US), Bernhard Zehrfuss (France) and Pier Luigi Nervi (Italy) and erected in 1958. Artists including Picasso, Jean Arp, Joan Miró and Henry Moore were commissioned to produce works for the building.

Map on page 47

Below: Les Invalides
Bottom: sculpture,
Palais Bourbon

LES INVALIDES

At the end of avenue de Breteuil are Les Invalides, comprising l'Esplanade des Invalides and the Hôtel des Invalides. ★★**L'Esplanade des Invalides** is a vast green square from where you have a fabulous view of the banks of the Seine, the superb Pont Alexandre III (built for the 1900 Universal Exhibition and distinguished by lavish gilding and decoration of cherubs) and the Grand and Petit Palais. Look out for the striking Art Deco Air France building.

The **Hôtel National des Invalides** ㉘ (open Oct–Mar 10am–5pm, till 6pm Apr–Sept, www.invalides.org) is a vast complex of buildings housing two churches, the ★★**Dome des Invalides** (inside which is the tomb of Napoleon I) and St-Louis-des-Invalides, and three museums: the ★ **Musée de l'Armée** (open Oct–Mar 10am–5pm, Apr–Sept till 6pm), the **Musée de l'Ordre de la Libération** and the **Musée des Plans Reliefs**. Now part of the Ministry of Defence but also occupied by a number of institutions belonging to other ministries, the Hôtel National des Invalides still retains its original function as a hospital and hospice. It commemorates the campaigns and battles that made French history.

The most important event in the history of the Invalides was the return of Napoleon's body. After seven years of negotiation with the British government, Louis-Philippe, King of France, obtained

permission to repatriate the Emperor's remains from St-Helena. On 8 October 1840, 19 years after Napoleon's death, the coffin was exhumed and opened for two minutes before transport to France aboard the frigate *La Belle Poule*. Reputedly, the body was perfectly preserved.

Star Attractions
● **Les Invalides**
● **Musée Rodin**
● **Assemblée Nationale**

MUSÉE RODIN

Next on this route is the delightful ★★★ **Musée Rodin** ㉙ (Apr–Sep daily except Mon, museum open 9.30am–5.45pm, park closes at 6.45pm, last admission 5.15pm; Oct–Mar museum open 9.30am–4.45pm, park closes at 5pm, last admission 4.15pm; free first Sun of month, www.penseur@musee-rodin.fr), containing the best of the sculptor's work and housed in the Hôtel Biron, his former home.

He came to live in the Hôtel Biron in 1908 and stayed there until his death in 1917. He paid his rent with money made from his best works; these form the basis of the museum's exquisite collection. Here are *The Kiss* (removed from the Chicago World Fair of 1893 for being too shocking), *The Thinker* (reputedly Dante contemplating the Inferno), *The Burghers of Calais*, *The Hand of God* and other works. Recently restored to their white marble finish, the statues ripple with life; many are set outside in delightful gardens. Also on show are works by Camille Claudel, the most famous of Rodin's many mistresses.

PALAIS BOURBON

The next stop is the ★★ **Assemblée Nationale – Palais Bourbon** ㉚ (33 bis quai d'Orsay; open Sat at 10am, 2pm, 3pm; closed during sessions; proof of identity required), which is the Lower House of the French Parliament. The extravagant columns were grafted on to an 18th-century façade by Napoleon to complement the church of La Madeleine across the river and now shelter an armed guard, protecting the 491 *députés* (Members of Parliament). Outside, the view from **Pont de la Concorde** is stunning.

> **Parisian underworld**
> The Parisian sewer is a complex network of 2,100km (1,300 miles) of tunnels built by Haussmann in the 19th century. In 1944 the Germans even set up offices in the sewers, with electricity, telephone and ventilation systems. You can visit the museum of Les Egouts de Paris (open Sat–Wed 11am–5pm, till 4pm in winter, closed last three weeks of Jan), which covers the history of the city's water and sewers from its origins to the present day.

One of the Burghers of Calais

Maps on page 47 and opposite

> **Les bouquinistes**
> A familiar sight along the banks of the Seine – and arguably as Parisian as the Eiffel Tower – are the riverside traders, known as the *bouquinistes*. Their wares – cards, posters and books – are displayed in make-shift, green boxes, which are locked up at night. Avoid the postcards and home in instead on the ancient, cellophane-wrapped books – many are second hand and can offer good value for money; you might even find a rare first edition.

Musée d'Orsay

5: Musée d'Orsay

France's national museum of 19th-century art, the ★★★ **Musée d'Orsay** ③ (open Tues, Wed, Fri–Sun 9am–6pm, Thur 9am–9.15pm in summer, Tues, Wed, Fri–Sat 10am–6pm, Sun 9am–6pm in winter; www.musee-orsay.fr) is housed in the former Gare d'Orsay, an ornate Beaux Arts train station designed by Victor Laloux. Opened in 1900 to serve passengers to the World Fair, it was built around a metal frame with a long, glass-roofed nave hidden behind an imposing stone façade – a triumph of modernity at that time, rivalling Eiffel's tower. However, in 1939 it ceased to serve mainline trains, as the platforms were too short for modern expresses. In 1977 President Giscard d'Estaing saved the building from demolition and declared that it would be converted into a new national museum, thus fulfilling the prophesy of the painter Edouard Detaille, who said at the opening ceremony in 1900 that the station would be better suited as a museum. Italian architect Gae Aulenti came up with the design for a skylit, central sculpture aisle along the line of the old tracks, inserting large internal partitions to create a series of rooms on either side. The Musée d'Orsay was finally opened to the public by Mitterrand in 1986.

THE COLLECTION

The museum's collection covers the period from 1848 to 1914. Although best known for its Impressionist works, the museum covers all key movements in later 19th-century French art, beginning with the late Romantics and official salon painters, and going via Realism, Impressionism and Symbolism to Post-Impressionism and the Nabis. Although overwhelmingly dominated by French painting, over the past few years those in charge at the Musée d'Orsay have been making an effort to acquire works by key European and American artists from the same period.

The collection also covers photography, presented in temporary exhibitions from the work of pioneers such as Fox Talbot, Daguerre and Niepce to portraits by Nadar, Muybridge's experiments with movement and photos by artistic amateurs such as Zola and Lewis Carroll.

The works are arranged on several levels around a vast central aisle, which makes a grand setting for sculpture by artists including David, Rodin and Maillol. Other artworks are shown

Star Attraction
● **Musée d'Orsay**

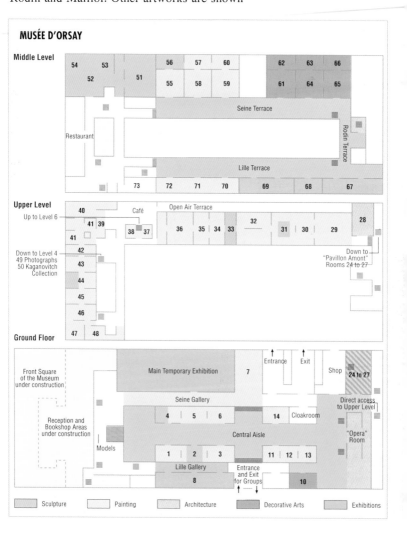

MUSÉE D'ORSAY

Middle Level

54 53 56 57 60 62 63 66
52 51 55 58 59 61 64 65

Seine Terrace

Restaurant

Rodin Terrace

Lille Terrace

73 72 71 70 69 68 67

Upper Level

40 Café Open Air Terrace
Up to Level 6
41 39 32 28
41 38 37 36 35 34 33 31 30 29
Down to Level 4 42
49 Photographs 43
50 Kaganovitch
Collection 44
45
46
47 48

Down to
"Pavillon Amont"
Rooms 24 to 27

Ground Floor

Entrance Exit Shop 24 to 27
Front Square
of the Museum Main Temporary Exhibition 7
under construction
Direct access
Seine Gallery to Upper Level
Reception and 4 5 6 14 Cloakroom "Opera"
Bookshop Areas Room
under construction Central Aisle
Models 1 2 3 11 12 13
Lille Gallery Entrance
8 and Exit 10
for Groups

Sculpture　　Painting　　Architecture　　Decorative Arts　　Exhibitions

Maps on pages 47 and 53

Below: Roses by Renoir
Bottom: Manet's Olympia

chronologically, starting on the ground floor. In room 1 are works by Ingres (notably ★ *La Source*), while in room 2 are the Romantic paintings of Delacroix including the tumultuous *Lion Hunt*, striking for its bold use of colour.

Much of the ground floor covers the Academic School and its regimented work, or *art pompier*, dominated by historical and mythological subjects. Cabanel's ★★ *Birth of Venus*, bought by Napoleon III in 1863, is a fine example of this. In contrast is Edouard Manet's nude ★★★ *Olympia* (1863), which was pronounced pornographic at the 1865 Paris salon and is considered to be the first 'modern' painting.

The visit continues on the upper floor with the museum's biggest draw, the ★★★ Impressionist paintings; here, they hang bathed in soft light from the station's glass-vaulted roof. Pass through galleries full of paintings by Monet, Manet, Renoir, Pissarro, Degas, Cézanne and Van Gogh. At the end is a small café under a large clock, from where a terrace high above the Seine offers appetising views over Paris.

Art nouveau overflows from the middle floor, including the two towers at the east end, which present a bird's-eye view of the museum. For more information on favourite works, visit the documentation room upstairs, where computers give details and video reproductions on all exhibits.

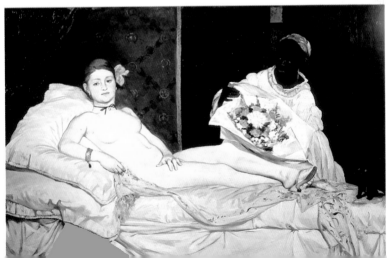

6: Trocadéro to Pont de l'Alma

The stretch from place du Trocadéro to place d'Iéna could be referred to as 'museum mile', such is its proliferation of exhibition spaces. Covering an impressive range of periods and media, from early Tibetan artifacts to fashion of the 1870s and cutting-edge installation art, the hotspots on this route should have something for every taste – just pick and choose. The route ends at the river – ideal for a trip on one of the famous Parisian riverboats.

Star Attractions
● **Musée d'Orsay**
● **Musée des Arts Asiatiques–Guimet**

PLACE DU TROCADÉRO

Cross the Seine to the ★ **place du Trocadéro ㉜**, from where there are magnificent views across to the Champ de Mars and the Eiffel Tower. Dominating the place du Trocadéro is the ★ **Palais de Chaillot ㉝**, built for the Paris World Fair of 1937. The imposing Art Deco palace was designed in the shape of an amphitheatre, with its wings following the original outline of the old Trocadéro in graceful symmetry. Much of the building is undergoing restoration and hence inaccessible. However, parts of the west wing, notably the **Musée de la Marine** (history of the French navy) and the **Musée de l'Homme** (prehistoric, anthropological and palaeontological collections) remain open. The latter will lose its ethnology collections in 2004 to the new Musée des Arts Premiers on quai Branly, near the Eiffel Tower.

The east wing of the restored Palais de Chaillot will house the former **Musée des Monuments Historiques**, to be renamed the **Cité de l'Architecture et du Patrimoine**. The Cité will be split into two sections, one on the classical and medieval periods, the other on the modern and contemporary ones.

The imposing Art Deco Palais de Chaillot

MUSÉE GUIMET

The route now heads east, down avenue Président Wilson towards the ★★ **Musée des Arts Asiatiques–Guimet ㉞** (6 place d'Iéna, open daily except Tues 10am–6pm, www.museeguimet.fr). This

Map on page 47

Below: 19th-century fashions from the Musée de la Mode
Bottom: street sign

museum, which reopened in 2001 after five years of extensive restoration, is home to an incredible number of sculptures, paintings and *objets d'art (*around 45,000 in total), based on the collection of the wealthy Lyon industrialist Emile Guimet. The collection illustrates the cultures and civilisations of Asia from the second millennium BC to the 19th century, and covers India and Southeast Asia (ground floor) and China, Japan, Korea, Nepal, Tibet and central Asia (upper floors).

PALAIS DE TOKYO

Further down the avenue du Président Wilson is the vast ★ **Palais de Tokyo** ㉟, built as the Electricity Pavilion for the 1937 World Fair. One wing was intended to hold fine art from post-1905 from the municipal fine art collection; the other wing (now the Site de Création Contemporaine, *see below*) was planned for the national collection of modern art, which was divided at that time between the Musée du Luxembourg and the Jeu de Paume.

However, plans changed due to World War II, after which the space was mostly used for temporary salons; the ★ **Musée d'Art Moderne de la Ville de Paris** (open Tues–Fri, 10am–5.30pm, Sat and Sun 10am–6.45pm) only opened in 1961. Then, in 1977, the core collection of French and international art was given a new home at the Pompidou Centre *(see page 75)*. The municipal

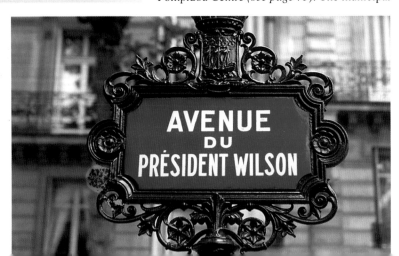

AVENUE DU PRÉSIDENT WILSON

collection of modern art that remained in the Palais de Tokyo has since been augmented by donations and purchases. While the emphasis at the Centre Pompidou is on international art, here the focus is on French artists and foreign émigrés who worked in Paris. Permanent and temporary exhibitions are held, with highlights including Matisse's ★★ *La Danse* and Raoul Dufy's ★★ *La Fée Electrique*. Note that major work is due to start in mid-2003 for around 12 months, during which time the museum will be closed.

In the opposite wing is the **Site de Création Contemporaine** (open Tues–Sun, noon–midnight, www.palaisdetokyo.com, free every first Sun of the month). Opened in January 2002, the centre is described as a 'laboratory for contemporary art'. An adventurous, multi-disciplinary programme focuses on the work of young artists, through exhibitions, performances and workshops.

MUSÉE DE LA MODE

Also in this area is the Parisian fashion museum, the ★ **Musée de la Mode de la Ville de Paris – Palais Galliera** ❸❻ (open daily except Mon 10am–5.40pm). The vast collection of more than 70,000 items, shown in changing exhibitions, covers French fashion and costume from the 18th century right up to the present day.

PONT DE L'ALMA AND THE RIVERBANK

From here, it's just a stroll to the **Pont de l'Alma**. The bridge, which was built in 1970 to replace one built by Napoleon III, rocketed into the limelight as the place of death of Princess Diana. Tourists still bring flowers to the entrance of the tunnel around the 'Liberty Flame', but this is not an official memorial. On the bridge, look for the 'Zouave', a statue of a soldier standing against one of the pillars. The statue is used as a river marker – if his toes get wet, Paris is put on flood alert. If his ankles go under water, roads adjacent to the river are closed, and if his hips are wet, an emergency floodplan is put into action across Paris.

Star Attraction
● Musée d'Art Moderne

Paris by boat

If you're near to Pont de l'Alma and fancy seeing Paris by boat, you could take the **Batobus** (quai de la Bourdonnais, tel: 01 44 11 33 99). The boat has eight stops: the Eiffel Tower, the Musée d'Orsay, St-Germain des Prés, Notre-Dame, the Jardin des Plantes, the Hôtel de Ville, the Louvre and the Champs-Elysées. It goes from 10am to 7pm April to Nov and 10am to 9pm from June to September and a boat leaves every 15–25 minutes. Alternatively, take one of the non-stop **Bâteaux-Mouches** (tel: 01 42 25 96 10) riverboats, which depart every 30 minutes from the Pont de l'Alma (length of the journey: around 1 hour 10 minutes).

One of the Bateaux-Mouches

Map opposite

Map opposite

Left Bank institutions
Close to the church of St-Germain-des-Prés are two Parisian literary institutions, the **Café de Flore** and **Les Deux Magots**. These archetypal Parisian cafés are famous as the meeting places for the 1960s' existentials, notably Jean-Paul Sartre and his partner Simone de Beauvoir. Although now somewhat overpriced, they do provide the ultimate Parisian café experience.

Boulevard St-Germain des Prés

7: St-Germain and the Latin Quarter

The Seine divides Paris in two, into the Rive Droite (Right Bank), the traditional centre of business and commerce, and the Rive Gauche (Left Bank), the stomping ground of the Parisian intelligentsia. This tour starts at the heart of the Rive Gauche, the chic boulevard St-Germain-des-Prés, before moving south and taking in Delacroix frescoes at St-Sulpice, flaura and fauna in the Jardin du Luxembourg and medieval masterpieces at the Musée National du Moyen Age–Thermes de Cluny. Also en route are the Sorbonne (Paris's elite university), the Panthéon mausoleum and the lively rue Mouffetard.

St-Germain-des-Prés

The boulevard St-Germain-des-Prés takes its name from St-Germain, cardinal of Paris in the 8th century. On his death he was buried in the 6th-century abbey of Ste-Croix-St-Vincent, now known as **St-Germain-des-Prés** ❸ (open daily 8am–7.30pm). The church has the oldest bell-tower in Paris and is the only Romanesque church that survived the 1789 revolution.

Musée Delacroix

From St-Germain-des-Prés it's just a hop north to 6 place Furstenberg and the ★ **Musée Eugène Delacroix** ❸ (open daily except Tues 9.30am–5.15pm), a small, attractive museum housed in one of the artist's former studios. (Delacroix lived here from 1857–63 while he was working on frescoes in the nearby church of St-Sulpice.) Temporary exhibitions are held in the airy former studio, while letters and personal effects are displayed in the house.

St-Sulpice

If the Musée Delacroix has whet your appetite for this artist's work, cross back over boulevard St-Germain and take rue Bonaparte towards place

St-Sulpice, the eastern side of which is dominated by Jean-Baptiste Servandoni's Italianesque church of the same name. **St-Sulpice ❸❾** is notable for its towers, one of which is higher than the other. Highlights inside include, in a chapel at the back of the church, Delacroix's massive oil-and-wax ★ **frescoes**, completed two years before his death.

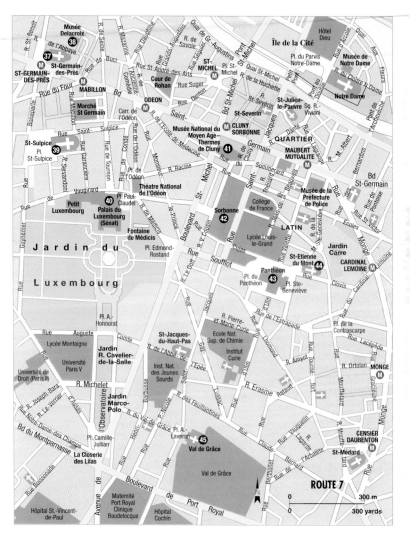

Map on page 59

*Below and bottom:
Left Bank literature*

JARDIN AND PALAIS DU LUXEMBOURG

It's a pleasant stroll along rue St-Sulpice towards the ★★ **Jardin du Luxembourg**. The gardens were extended and laid out in their present-day form by Chalgrin at the end of the 18th century. The southernmost end of the park is rounded off by Carpeaux's ★ **Fontaine de l'Observatoire**, on which female figures represent the four continents.

North of the park is the **Palais du Luxembourg** ⓸⓪, built for Marie de Médicis after the murder of her husband Henri IV. The widowed queen moved into the palais in 1625, when it was still unfinished. She left the neighbouring Petit Palais *(see page 42)* to Richelieu, who was to become her enemy – in 1631, with the support of her son Louis XIII, he forced her into exile, and she died in Cologne in 1642, lonely and embittered. The Palais du Luxembourg remained a royal palace until the Revolution; since 1800 it has housed the French Senate, the country's highest legislative body.

The former Musée du Luxembourg (next to the palace) is now a gallery housing temporary exhibitions. The adjacent Petit Luxembourg is the official home of the president of the Senate.

MUSEE NATIONAL DU MOYEN AGE

A short walk northeast of the Jardin du Luxembourg is the ★★ **Musée National du Moyen Age – Thermes de Cluny** ⓸⓵ (open daily except Tues 9.15am–5.45pm, free first Sun of the month, www.musee-moye-nage.fr), a sumptuous collection of medieval tapestries, sculpture and precious artefacts housed in the former palace of the abbots of Cluny.

The most famous work in the collection is the *Lady and the Unicorn* tapestry cycle; five of its panels depict an allegory of the senses, while the meaning of the sixth panel remains undetermined. Other highlights in the museum include glass from Sainte-Chapelle, statues of the Kings of Judah (*c*1220) from Notre-Dame, and Roman heating and sauna systems discovered under the palace. Also of note are the Cour d'Honneur, the open-air ruins of Gallo-Roman thermal baths and the medieval-style garden, created in 2000.

THE SORBONNE

Nearby, on rue St-Jacques, is the vast complex of the **Sorbonne** ❷ (entrance at 47 rue des Ecoles). Now the largest university in France, it was founded in 1257 by Robert de Sorbon, chaplain to Louis IX, as a college offering education and accommodation to impoverished theology students. The institute grew in size and reputation until its name was transferred to the University of Paris in the 19th century.

THE PANTHEON

At the end of rue Soufflot is the huge domed ★★ **Panthéon** ❸ (open daily summer 9.30am–6.30pm, winter 10am to 6.30pm), which stands on the small rise of the ancient Mons Luticius, consecrated to the patron saint of Paris, Ste-Geneviève, in the Middle Ages. In 1756 the foundation stone for the ambitious new building, modelled on St Peter's in Rome, was laid. The design was the masterpiece of architect, Jacques-Germain Soufflot, who died ten years before its completion in 1791.

Almost immediately after the building was finished, the revolutionary authorities decided to make the church a last resting place for heroes of the revolution. Voltaire's mortal remains were transferred to the Panthéon crypt that same year. He was followed not only by Jean-Jacques

Star Attractions
● Jardin du Luxembourg
● Musée National du Moyen Age
● Panthéon

The existentialists
The freedom of the period post World War II was characterised in Paris by an outpouring of literature and ideas. One of the most notable philosophies to emerge was existentialism, developed by Jean-Paul Sartre and based on the concept of a meaningless, or absurd, universe, in which people were meant to find freedom by assuming greater personal responsibilities. In trying to change, rather than simply examine, the world, existentialism represented a hope for the future. Key figures included Sartre's companion, Simone de Beauvoir, and the novelist Albert Camus.

Parisian institution

Map on page 59

Rousseau, Victor Hugo and Emile Zola, but also by the remains of the World War II Resistance leader Jean Moulin, for whom a symbolic tomb was built in the 1970s. Most recent additions to the Panthéon include the remains of Pierre and Marie Curie (1995) and of André Malraux (1996), culture minister under de Gaulle.

In addition to viewing the tombs, visitors can see Foucault's Pendulum, which hangs permanently from the interior roof of the Dome, and the 19th-century frescoes by symbolist painter Puvis de Chavanne.

Student riots, May 1968

The 1968 agitation began in March with a sit-in by students who demanded changes in the antiquated university system. The riot police were called in, and on 10 May they stormed 60 barricades in the Quartier Latin. Unrest spread to the factories and other cities, France was soon paralysed, and Paris was left in a state of siege. Petrol was rationed and canny housewives hoarded food.

At the end of May, de Gaulle announced elections, warning against totalitarianism. The Parisian bourgeoisie awoke, and an hour later over 500,000 de Gaulle supporters marched down the Champs-Elysées. The Gaullists won the election, but glory was short-lived: de Gaulle resigned in 1969.

ST-ETIENNE-DU-MONT

Behind the Panthéon, in rue St-Etienne-du-Mont, is the church of ★ **St-Etienne-du-Mont** ④ (open 9am–7.30pm, closed noon–2pm on Sat, Sun and Mon in July and August). This used to be the parish church of the Abbey of Ste-Geneviève and still houses a shrine to the city's patron saint. The real highlight is the ★★ **Renaissance rood screen** (1541), the only rood screen in Paris.

RUE MOUFFETARD

The road running south of St-Etienne-du-Mont is rue Mouffetard, known locally as 'la Mouff'. This Roman road, one of the oldest streets in Paris,

1968 student riots

is the site of an excellent food market (every Sat until 1.30pm). At No 101, the Passage des Patriarches (or the Passage des Postes at No 104) leads to **place de la Contrescarpe**, one of the prettiest squares in Paris, where Rabelais, Verlaine and the Pléiade poets used to meet. Café Delmas is a good choice for a coffee.

ARENES DE LUTECE

At the southern end of rue Mouffetard is place Monge; from here take rue Monge as far as the Arènes de Lutèce. The Roman settlement of Lutetia built an amphitheatre here cAD200, but after the barbarian invasion in 285 it was used as a quarry; it was only in the reign of Napoeon III when rue Monge was created that the ruins were found.

The amphitheatre (open 10am–dusk) covers an area of 100m (330ft) by 130m (425ft) – almost as large as the great amphitheatre in Nîmes. Tiered seating provided places for 15,000 spectators to watch gladiators, plays or circus performances.

VAL-DE-GRACE

Now head southwest in the direction of rue St-Jacques and the church of **Val-de-Grâce** ㊺. Anne of Austria had vowed to build the church if she bore a son, and after the safe birth of the future Louis XIV, the commission went to architect François Mansart. His original plans were altered by his successor on the scheme, Jacques Lemercier.

The building's façade is celebrated for its architectural harmony, despite the immensity of the dome at the rear. Mansart's interior shows a strong Italian influence: the nave and the central building form a unity, and the majestic dome room, where the choir and the huge transepts meet, is an extension of the main hall. The colourful flooring is highly decorative, and its pattern harmonises with that of the barrel vault above. There is a large baldachin altar with barley-sugar columns beneath the dome. The monastery building contains a cloister, a school for army doctors and, attached to it, a medical museum.

Star Attraction
● **Rood screen,
St-Etienne-du-Mont**

*Below: the Panthéon
Bottom: cheese,
rue Mouffetard market*

Map
below

8: Opéra and Grands Boulevards

This route provides a busy day of sightseeing and window-shopping in one of the grandest shopping areas of the city. It starts and ends with monuments erected to the glory of Napoleon I – not uncommon sights in the great conquerer's former capital. From La Madeleine, one of Paris's most stately churches, the tour heads northwest towards the chocolate-box Second Empire opera house and the surrounding Grands Boulevards, laid out by Baron Haussmann in the 19th century. Here, you'll find a concentration of department stores and chain stores, making this one of the best places in Paris for one-stop shopping. Heading further south, we pass through elegant arcades towards the upmarket Faubourg St-Honoré, home to a string of chic designer stores and elegant cafés. Pick and choose from the route according to how long you want to dedicate to sightseeing and how much time you'd spend in the shops.

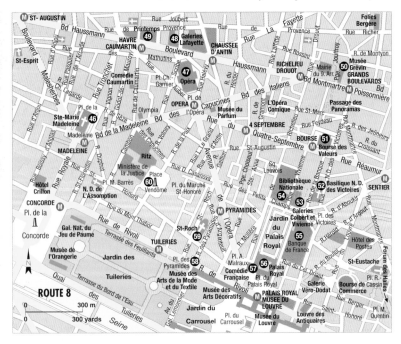

LA MADELEINE

Start at the Métro station Concorde with a stroll along the elegant **rue Royale**; look out for Ladurée at No 16 – this French institution is a great place for breakfast. Now make for the **place de la Madeleine**, dominated by the church of **Ste-Marie-Madeleine** ⑯. In 1764, Louis XV laid the foundation stone for the present structure, which initially was intended to resemble the Panthéon. Building was slow, and in 1805 Napoleon decided to turn the half-finished church into a Temple of Glory for his Grande Armée. In 1808 the structure assumed its present neo-classical appearance, but work stopped on it after the fall of Napoleon; the church was only finally consecrated in 1845. The bare, uninviting interior is in the shape of a long hall vaulted by three domes. The apse contains a romantic neoclassical fresco, showing Christ, St Madeleine and historical figures including Napoleon.

Place de la Madeleine is also home to luxury shops, including Fauchon, nicknamed 'millionaire's supermarket', owing to the 20,000 goods it sells from across the globe, Hédiard chocolatiers and truffle retailers Maison de la Truffe. Also on the square is the **Kiosk-Théâtre de la Madeleine**, where you can buy half-price seats for same-day theatre shows across Paris. A flower market is held in the square from Tuesday to Friday.

L'OPERA

The route now continues along boulevard de la Madeleine and boulevard des Capucines (where the composer Jacques Offenbach died at No 8 in 1880) towards **place de l'Opéra**. This broad square is dotted with elegant shops and cafés, notably the Café de la Paix, one of the city's best-known meeting-points for politicians and the literati during the Belle Epoque.

The city's opera house, the ★★ **Opéra National de Paris – Palais Garnier** ⑰ (open daily 12.45–1.45pm; guided tours in English, Tues–Sun 1pm and 2pm), soars over the north end of the square. Built between 1862–75 on the orders of

Star Attraction
● Opéra Garnier

Below: Printemps department store
Bottom: gilded statue on the Palais Garnier

Map on page 64

Napoleon III and to the sum of almost 50 million francs, the opera house, designed by previously unknown architect Charles Garnier, is the finest structure of the Second Empire. Opera and ballet are now performed both here and at the more contemporary Opéra de la Bastille *(see page 80)*.

On the outside of the building, enormous sculptured groups adorn the front and corners of the façade, the highest of which shows Apollo with his lyre. Medallions and gilded bronze busts depict important composers. Inside the house there is further opulence. Marble statues of the composers Lully, Rameau, Gluck and Handel adorn the vestibule, and beyond them are halls of mirrors and foyers, all of them elaborate. The large stairway (Escalier d'Honneur) that leads from the entrance floor to the first balcony is the entire width of the auditorium. The five-storey horseshoe auditorium, decorated in Italian style, contains nearly 2,000 seats, though 258 of them provide only a limited view of the stage. The intense colours of the auditorium's ceiling, painted by Marc Chagall in 1964, blend harmoniously with the red and gold of the interior.

Below: traditional cartes postales
Bottom: Palais Garnier

LES GRANDS MAGASINS

The area just behind the Opera House, along boulevard Haussmann, is dominated by the 'grands magasins' (department stores), notably ★★ **Galeries**

Lafayette **48** and ★★ **Au Printemps 49**, both established in the late 19th century and rivals since then. At the turn of the 20th century these palatial new emporia of fashion and novelties brought hitherto unimagined choice to shoppers. Recently, considerable investment has been made on revamping their image and on refurbishments, spurred on by competition from such up-and-coming lifestyle stores as Colette, on nearby rue St-Honoré. Galeries Lafayette is especially famed for its splendid 25-m (82-ft) high art nouveau central hall topped with a vast coloured-glass dome.

Star Attractions
● **Galeries Lafayette**
● **Printemps**

BOULEVARDS AND BACK STREETS

If your appetite for one-stop shopping is sated, make for boulevard des Capucines, which soon turns into boulevard des Italiens. At the top of the road, turn right onto boulevard Montmartre, home to several of Paris's delightful covered arcades; passage Jouffroy is on the left as you head west.

Just after passage Jouffroy is rue du Faubourg Montmartre, where at No 7 you can enjoy a cheap lunch at Chartier, a popular, traditional bistro offering inexpensive French food. Back on the main boulevard is the **Musée Grevin 50** (boulevard de Montmartre 10; open daily 1–7pm, www.grevin.com), a restored wax museum containing around 300 effigies of contemporary personalities as well as historic scenes. The museum's art nouveau Théâtre Joli is particularly lovely.

Head right down rue Notre-Dame des Victoires, past another 19th-century arcade, the Passage des Panoramas, towards **place de la Bourse** and the **Bourse 51**, (open Mon–Fri 1.15–4pm by appointment only, tel: 01 40 41 62 20, www.bourse-de-paris.fr) or Stock Exchange. The grand building is one of the most distinctive of the Napoleonic era.

Take the narrow Passage des Petits-Pères leading to place de Petits-Pères and the **Basilique Notre-Dame des Victoires 52**. Construction on the church began in 1629 but was interrupted numerous times before the church was finally finished in 1740. In the second chapel is the thumb of Lully, the King's court composer.

> 👁 **Napoleon III-style**
> When architect Charles Garnier's over-elaborate design won a competition mounted by Napoleon III for a new opera house, the emperor's wife, Eugénie, supposedly asked him what style his building was in. 'What is this style, it is neither Greek nor Louis XVI?'. 'No,' replied Garnier, 'it is Napoleon III style'.

Detail from Marc Chagall's ceiling at the Opéra Garnier

Map on page 64

Below: stylish shopping
Bottom: the interior of the
Galeries Lafayette

Galeries Colbert and Vivienne

On rue des Petits Champs are the early 19th-century aristocratic, covered arcades **Galerie Colbert** and **Galerie Vivienne** ㉝. Recently renovated, both arcades hint at past grandeur, fitted out with intricate brass lamps, graceful glass canopies and marbled mosaic floors. Sip a strong coffee at the expansive copper counter of the refurbished Le Grand Colbert, an 1830s brasserie at 4 rue Vivienne and pop into No 6 to check out Jean-Paul Gaultier's latest creations. Tea addicts will find a welcome repose at A Priori Thé, in the Galerie Vivienne, a *salon de thé* that spreads out into the gallery.

Bibliotheque Nationale Richelieu

Parallel to rue Vivienne is rue Richelieu, where, at No 58 is the ★★ **Bibliothèque Nationale de France – Richelieu** ㉞ (open Tues–Sat 1–5pm, Sun and holidays 12pm–6pm, closed two weeks in Sept; www.bnf.fr). Formerly home to every book published in France since 1500, most of the collection has now been rehoused in the massive, ultra-modern premises at Tolbiac – the last of Mitterrand's *grands projets*. The library's book collection is one of the biggest in the world and includes Charlemagne's illuminated bible and original manuscripts from Villon, Rabelais, Hugo and Proust. The Richelieu building is keeping the specialised departments of

prints, drawings, maps, music and manuscripts. The main reading room, designed by Henri Labrouste in 1863, is an architectural masterpiece. Downstairs, the permanent museum, **Cabinet des Médailles et Antiques** (open afternoons; entrance fee), contains *objets d'art* from the royal collections seized during the Revolution.

Opposite the library, across rue Richelieu, is the lovely small **square Louvois**, containing one of the most beautiful fountains in Paris, which represents the four 'female' rivers of France – La Loire, La Seine, La Garonne and La Saône.

BANQUE DE FRANCE

On rue de Valois (reached via rue des Petits Champs) lies the **Banque de France** 🕔 (open on *Journées du Patrimoine, see page 78*, only). The oldest part of this complex is the Palais des Ducs de la Vrillière, built by Mansart between 1635 and 1638. During the Revolution the national printing works were housed here; since 1811 it has been the headquarters of the Banque de France.

JARDIN DU PALAIS-ROYAL

On the other side of rue de Valois there are several ways through to the **Jardin du Palais-Royal**, a real oasis of tranquillity in the midst of all the big-city bustle. It was not always so peaceful, however. This garden used to be a meeting-point for agitators during the French Revolution: two days before the storming of the Bastille, the journalist Desmoulins issued his call to arms to the citizens here. It was from a trader in the Palais-Royal in 1793 that Charlotte Corday bought the knife with which she stabbed Marat in his bath. Jean Cocteau lived for years in an apartment in Galerie Montpensier. Colette, one of the most Parisian of novelists, died in Galerie Beaujolais in 1954.

Behind the gardens are contemporary artist Daniel Buren's striking black-and-white columns (Colonnes de Buren), which caused great controversy when first unveiled in 1986.

Star Attraction
● Bibliothèque Nationale de France–Richelieu

Place des Victoires
Adjacent to the Banque de France and Galeries Colbert and Vivienne is the place de Victoires, an archetypal Royal square designed in 1685 by Louis XIV's architect Jules-Hardouin Mansart. The first square dedicated to Louis XIV, the *place* was built as an open-air room with a statue of the Sun King in its centre. The square became a model for many squares across France.

Galerie Vivienne

Map on page 64

PALAIS-ROYAL

Cardinal Richelieu, appointed prime minister in 1624, commissioned Jacques Lemercier to build a *hôtel particulier* near the Louvre. A few years later, after the adjacent city wall had been pulled down, the cardinal had the building converted into a large residence (1634–9), known as the Palais Cardinal. On his death in 1642, Richelieu left the palace to the crown, and it became the childhood home of Louis XIV, as the ★★ **Palais-Royal** ⑤⑥

At the beginning of the 18th century the dukes of Orléans took up residence here. The palace was turned into a den of debauchery through the infamous 'libertine dinners' held by Philippe d'Orléans. Gambling and prostitution were rife, as the police were banned from entering the palace.

In 1780, to compensate for his family's free spending, Louis-Philippe built shops in the galleries around the palace and let them at exorbitant prices – hence the proliferation of arcaded galleries in this area.

After the revolution, this complex with its restaurants and casinos became the focal point of Parisian life, until the Palais fell to the Orléans once again after the demise of Napoleon. The Palais-Royal was damaged during the Paris Commune (1871), but was then faithfully reconstructed by Chabrol (1872–6). The galleries still contain several second-hand bookshops, philately shops and restaurants.

Breakfast or brunch in a palace
In the area covered in this chapter, there are several hotels housed within former palaces. For a treat why not have breakfast or brunch there. Le Bristol is at 12 rue du Faubourg Saint-Honoré, the Ritz – where Coco Chanel lived in a three-room suite – is on place Vendôme, and the Crillon is just a stone's throw away on the place de la Concorde.

Columns by Daniel Buren, Palais-Royal

COMÉDIE FRANÇAISE

Right next to the Palais-Royal is the **Comédie Française** ⑤⑦ (entrance on place Colette). On the eastern side of the square is the monument to the poet and dramatist Alfred de Musset (1810–75). The Duke of Orléans, Philippe-Egalité, had this theatre constructed according to plans by Victor Louis (1786–90), and it was given its present-day façade by Prosper Chabrol in 1867. Since 1799 it has been the headquarters of France's national theatre, the Comédie Française, formed in 1680 when several smaller theatre groups merged with the ensemble of the French playwright Molière. Less than a year later, Louis XIV designated the building his court theatre, and Napoleon Bonaparte made it his state theatre. The productions staged here today are mostly taken from the classical repertoire.

The theatre's foyer contains the chair in which Molière was sitting in 1673 during a performance of his play *Le Malade Imaginaire* (The Hypochondriac) when he collapsed. The audience believed that this was all part of the act – an old man feigns death in the play – and responded with enthusiasm; tragically, this was not the case, and the great dramatist died later the same day.

Star Attraction
● Palais Royal

Below: Molière
Bottom: Comédie Française

LOUVRE DES ANTIQUAIRES

The route continues west along rue de Rivoli, past the **Louvre des Antiquaires,** home to some 250 antiques dealers. At 224 rue de Rivoli is Galignani, a bookshop established in the 16th century; at No 226 is the lovely art nouveau *salon de thé* Angelina, at No 228 is the grand Hôtel Meurice, headquarters of the German Army during the Occupation and at No 248 is a large branch of WH Smith, the biggest English bookshop in France.

PLACE DES PYRAMIDES

Continuing west, you reach the small **place des Pyramides** ⑤⑧. In the middle of the square is a gleaming golden equestrian statue of **Joan of Arc,** placed on the site where, according to legend, the

Map on page 64

Famous Rivoli residents
Rue de Rivoli attracted a number of famous residents including the Russian novelist Ivan Turgenev (1818–83), who lived here with his daughter (at No 210) and French author and playwright Alexandre Dumas (1802– 70), who resided at No 22 in 1836. In 1944 General von Choltitz, placed in charge of Paris by Hitler, set up his headquarters in the Hôtel Meurice (rue de Rivoli 228). The general prevented the destruction of the city by refusing to carry out the Führer's orders for all the bridges, monuments and important buildings in the city to be blown up during the German retreat.

Gilded Joan of Arc on the place des Pyramides

Maid of Orléans was wounded in 1429 during the Paris siege. There is a procession to this statue on All Saints' Day every year. Nowadays Joan is sadly a cult figure for the Right Wing, notably the National Front. At No 2 is the Hôtel Régina, a fine example of art nouveau decoration.

ST-ROCH

Running parallel to rue de Rivoli is rue St-Honoré. At No 296 is the church of **St-Roch** ❺ (open daily 8.15am–7.30pm). Louis XIV laid the foundation-stone for this church in 1653, and the building was consecrated to the patron saint of plague victims (St Roch). St Roch was once the finest baroque church in all Paris, but most of its fine sculpture and façade decoration was lost in the Revolution. Nevertheless the church still owns a rich collection of excellent religious works of art, brought there in 1819 from demolished Paris churches. It is also the resting place of France's most celebrated, landscape gardener, André Le Nôtre.

On 5 October 1795 several rebellious royalists who had barricaded themselves into the church were summarily shot on the church steps on the orders of Napoleon Bonaparte. Bulletholes and other traces from the battle can be seen on the church wall.

PLACE VENDOME

Head along rue St-Honoré and turn right into rue Castiglione to reach ★★ **place Vendôme** ⑥⓪, the architectural heart of one of Paris's most elegant quarters, the distinguished Faubourg St-Honoré. The square dates back to the reign of Louis XIV, when the King, delighted with the recently constructed place des Victoires *(see page 69)* instructed Mansart to build a second square.

According to the original plans, today's place Vendôme was to have been a royal square with a statue of the king at its centre, surrounded by public buildings; it was initially to be known as place Louis-le-Grand. Work began on the façades in 1687, but buyers could not be found for the strips of land behind them. In 1699 an equestrian statue of the king was erected. The completion of the square thus dragged on until 1720.

The monument in the middle of the square closely reflects French history. In 1792, during the Revolution, the statue of Louis XIV was destroyed, and Napoleon had the 45-m (150-ft) high **Colonne de la Grande Armée** (Triumphal Column), decorated with reliefs commemorating his glorious campaigns, placed there instead.

The bronze used to make the statue was taken from 1,200 pieces of enemy cannon captured during the various battles. A statue of Napoleon stood at the top of the column, but Napoleon III found it too small and had it replaced by the Roman-style imperial one up there today. In 1871 the column was pulled down by Communard insurrectionists. Since the painter Gustave Courbet was suspected of having had a hand in the deed, he paid for the monument's re-erection out of his own pocket.

Place Vendôme has survived revolution and insurrection with remarkably litle damage. Today it is the home of wealthy bankers and exclusive jewellers, of which Cartier is probably the best known. At No 15 is the elegant Ritz Hotel, founded at the end of the 19th century and infamous as the venue for the last dinner of Princess Diana and Dodi al-Fayed in August 1997. The Ministry of Justice is located in the square, and the composer Frédéric Chopin died at No 12 in 1849.

Star Attraction
● **Place Vendôme**

Below: place Vêndome
Bottom: famous restaurant

Map below

9: Around the Centre Pompidou

This route covers a small area in the centre of Paris that has caused more than its fair share of architectural controversy over the years. The major site en route is the Centre Pompidou, once considered an eyesore but now greatly loved, with statistics to match – it attracts nearly 8 million visitors a year, making it the most-visited cultural site in the world. It's advisable to allow at least a couple of hours to visit the centre's excellent art gallery. Also en route are the complex of Les Halles and the historic Hôtel de Ville (town hall), where Parisian passions have raged over the centuries, for hangings, revolts and national celebrations. Much of this area is pedestrianised, making it a pleasant place to stroll or to sit at a pavement café and watch the world go by.

Fountain of Innocents

The Fontaine des Innocents, the only remaining Renaissance fountain in Paris, is located on the site of the city's former cemetery, Les Innocents, southeast of Les Halles. By the 18th century, the graveyard had become a putrid necropolis, as the dead were carried there among produce bound for the market at Les Halles. The cemetery was finally closed, and its contents moved to the catacombs (*see page 93*). Today, the square is a meeting place for the city's youth.

LES HALLES

This part of Paris has been a commercial area since 1183, when Philippe-Auguste erected permanent market halls and ordered the city traders to close

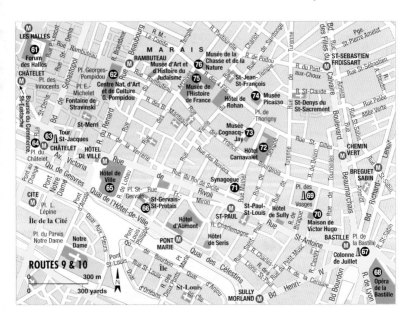

their shops for two days a week to do business at his own market. Under Napoleon III the market was rebuilt as 10 iron halls, which resembled small railway stations; these were fed by vast underground storehouses, dark kingdoms of death and decay, where cages of animals were piled amongst rotting fruits, ruled over by weak-sighted storekeepers. Up above, stallholders, restaurant owners, pickpockets, artists, prostitutes and police crowded the market halls.

The last night of the market, Thursday 27 February 1969, was a sad occasion for Parisians. The animated halls, lovingly described by Emile Zola (1840–1902) in his novel *Le Ventre de Paris (The Belly of Paris)*, were deemed no longer suitable for 20th-century commerce, and trading was moved to the suburb of Rungis, near Orly Airport.

The market site became popularly known as *le trou des Halles (trou* = hole), since it remained unused until the early 1980s. Eventually, the **Forum des Halles ➏**, a faceless underground shopping centre, was built here. Above ground are glass-and-steel mushrooms housing cultural centres for contemporary arts and poetry, the Pavillon des Arts and Maison de la Poésie.

Not far away, on the edge of the Forum des Halles (1 rue du Jour), is the church of **St-Eustache**. Work started on this place of worship in 1532, owing to a generous grant from François I, and it became Paris' first Renaissance building.

CENTRE POMPIDOU

East of Les Halles, along rue Rambuteau, is the **★★★ Centre National d'Art et de Culture Georges Pompidou ➋** (open Mon and Wed–Sun 11am–10pm, closed Tues; note that the galleries close at 9pm; www.centrepompidou.fr), a dynamic arts venue and Paris's main showcase for modern and contemporary art. The centre was built by architects Richard Rogers, Renzo Piano and Gianfranco Franchini at the request of ex-president Pompidou – hence the name – and its inside-out design, dominated by external pipes, tubes, scaffolds and escalators, caused extreme controversy

Star Attraction
● Centre Pompidou

Below: Café Beaubourg
Bottom: Centre Pompidou

Tour St-Jacques

when it was unveiled in 1977. However, the pipes are not just for show: the blue ones convey air, the green ones carry water, the yellow ones contain the electrics, and the red ones conduct heating. The slightly sunken forecourt provides a perfect stage for street entertainment.

The centre underwent extensive renovation for the millennium – the entrance hall and ticket office were extended, an educational area was created and the Bibliothèque Publique d'Information, a large public library, was housed within the centre. Also incorporated into the complex are a performance space, auditorium and cinema, and adjacent is the avant-garde music institute IRCAM.

However, the main attraction for visitors is the **Musée National de l'Art Moderne**, situated on the fourth and fifth floors. The 5,000-strong collection is already far too big to be shown in full here – and it's still growing – but regular rehangs are intended to enable regular visitors to see as much of the collection as possible.

The fifth floor covers the modern period, from 1905 up to the 1960s, with highlights including works by Picasso, Matisse, Kandinsky, Klee, Klein and Pollock, and sections on Dadaism and Surrealism. The fourth floor is devoted to the centre's excellent contemporary collection, incorporating work from the 1960s to the present day. Here, visitors can admire work by artists including Andy Warhol, Xavier Veilhan, Claude Viallat, Verner Panton, Joseph Beuys, Gerhard Richter and Jean Dubuffet. Displays of 20th-century design and architecture, as well as installations, are now interspersed among the paintings. Temporary exhibitions are shown on level six. (Also on the sixth floor is the fashionable, minimalist Georges restaurant, tel: 01 44 78 47 99.)

Included within the price of the museum ticket is a visit to a reconstruction of sculptor Constantin Brancusi's studio, **l'Atelier Brancusi**. And if that whets your appetite for sculpture, look out for the **Fontaine de Stravinsky**, at the southern end of the Centre Pompidou. The fountain features brightly coloured, spindly, spouting forms, each named after music by the Russian composer.

Map on page 74

TOUR ST-JACQUES

Now walk southwest to the square St-Jacques and its lofty **Tour St-Jacques** ⓺. This Gothic tower (1508–22) is all that remains of the parish church that was once the spiritual centre of the densely populated Châtelet *quartier*. Both the church and the rue St-Jacques – which runs through the Latin Quarter on the opposite bank of the Seine – are named after St James; they are reminders that this route was once heavily travelled by medieval pilgrims heading for Santiago de Compostela in Spain, to visit the tomb of the saint. Look out for the statue of scientist and philospher Blaise Pascal (1623–62) who carried out experiments on atmospheric pressure from the top.

PLACE DU CHATELET

To the east of the Tour St-Jacques is **place du Châtelet** ⓺. The name commemorates the bulwark known as the Grand Châtelet that was set up at the head of the bridge in 1130 to monitor pedestrian traffic over the river to the Ile de la Cité. Deprived of its function in 1109, when Philippe Auguste built the city wall, the Châtelet then became the official residence of the Provost of Paris – the latter was appointed by the king to keep an eye on law and order, and remained so until the function was abolished in 1790 as a

La Samaritaine
If time allows, take a short stroll northwest along the Seine from place du Châtelet towards La Samaritaine, one of the biggest and oldest department stores in Paris. (The shop is spread over five buildings, joined by overhead walkways.) On the roof of the second building, which has an Art Nouveau façade, the terrace restaurant offers one of the finest views of Paris – at a reasonable price.

A sign of political independence

Map on page 74

result of the Revolution. In 1800 the theatre buildings opposite were built by Davioud: the Théâtre du Châtelet and Théâtre de la Ville.

HOTEL DE VILLE

Opening out at the eastern end of avenue Victoria is the wide esplanade fronting the ★★ **Hôtel de Ville** ❻ (guided tours Mon only; tel: 01 42 76 50 46). This broad square, now called the **place de l'Hôtel de Ville**, was once known as the place de Grève (*grève* means beach) and was used for the loading and unloading of Seine shipping in the Middle Ages. From 1310 until 1830 the square was used for public executions and for meetings among the city's unemployed (the French term for 'to go on strike' is *faire la grève*).

The square has long been the site of the city's town hall. Under François I the largely dilapidated first such building was replaced by a design built in 1533 by the Italian Domenico da Cortana (known as Bocador), who had already made a name for himself designing the Loire *châteaux* at Chambord and Blois. The building was not completed until 1628 because of the Wars of Religion. During the 1871 Paris Commune it was destroyed by fire, but it was reconstructed in its original form, and with a splendid Mansard roof and decoration of bare-breasted maidens, between 1873 and 1882. This square was the scene of great celebrations on the Liberation of Paris in 1944.

ST-GERVAIS-ST-PROTAIS

To the east of the Hôtel de Ville lies the church of **St-Gervais-St-Protais** ❼. Work began on its construction in 1494, but it was not completed until the early 17th century. The façade (1616–17) was revolutionary for its time – although Salomon de Brossé modelled it on the Roman baroque façade, its three storeys of double pillars lend it a particular severity. Owing to its sparseness of detail it is considered one of the earliest examples of French Classicism, although the interior is predominantly Late Gothic.

Open house
Since 1984 France has held 'Journées du Patrimoine' – open house days – on which otherwise inaccessible sites of national heritage, including churches, town halls, abbeys, and former private mansions, are open to the public. In Paris, sights include the Hôtel de Ville, Palais de l'Elysée and Banque de France. For the majority of sites, entry is free, but for some venues identification (a passport or identity card) needs to be shown.

Pounding the Parisian backstreets

10: Bastille and Marais

The Bastille, a familiar name with its place ensured in the history books as the starting place of the Revolution, was for many years rather run down and uninteresting. The construction of a glitzy new opera house here in 1989 sparked regeneration in the area, and the streets around place de la Bastille are now known for their hip boutiques, trendy bars and cutting-edge galleries.

The Marais (literally 'swamp') was transformed in the 16th century from a stretch of muddy farmland into the centre of Parisian society. When in the 1680s the aristocrats left the grand homes they had built here to follow Louis XIV to his new royal palace at Versailles, the area degenerated. It was not until the 1960s that renovation began, and by the 1990s the Marais was once again one of the most sought-after addresses in Paris. Chic boutiques and hip cafés sit side-by-side with some of the city's best museums, and the area's narrow streets make a trip here a delight.

Star Attractions
● **Hôtel de Ville**
● **place de la Bastille**

Below: Opéra de la Bastille
Bottom: Délacroix's Liberty
Leading the People

PLACE DE LA BASTILLE

Start at ★★ **place de la Bastille** ❻, which takes its name from a bulwark, known as *la petite Bastille* (the little bastion), erected here in the 14th century by Charles V. However, the fortress's

Map on page 74

Below: Victor Hugo
Bottom: place des Vosges

military role was slight – it withstood just one of seven sieges during the civil wars – and under Henri IV it was used to store the state treasure.

Under Richelieu the Bastille was converted into a prison, where Voltaire and the Marquis de Sade were among its famous inmates. On 14 July 1789 the storming of the Bastille marked the start of the French Revolution. At first the mob surrounded the building because they assumed it housed arms and ammunition. When long negotiation between the rebels and the commander proved fruitless, the prison was stormed, and the commander and nine soldiers beheaded; the seven remaining prisoners (four counterfeiters, two madmen and a young aristocrat) were freed. The demolition of the Bastille began the next day.

At the centre of the place de la Bastille is the **Colonne de Juillet**, erected in 1840. This 47-m (154-ft) high victory column, made of bronze in the shape of a huge tombstone, commemorates not the 1789 Revolution but the victims of the July Revolution of 1830, who are buried beneath it.

OPERA DE LA BASTILLE

Dominating the square is the ★★**Opéra de la Bastille ㊽**, designed by Carlos Ott and opened on 14 July on the 200-year anniversary of the Revolution. One of Mitterrand's *grands projets (see*

page 91), the opera house has room for 2,700 spectators and was intended to bring traditionally elitist arts to the masses. Its popularist programme and the premature deterioration of the building have earned much critical disdain, but the house has enjoyed commercial success nonetheless.

Star Attractions
● **Opéra de la Bastille**
● **place des Vosges**

THE MARAIS

Now walk west, along rue St-Antoine, then turn right into rue de Birague towards the Marais, home to one of Paris's most attractive squares, the focal point of the city's Jewish population and home to several major museums. It's also a great place to shop or stop for a coffee, lunch or dinner.

Viaduc des Arts
Built in 1859, the Viaduc de Paris supported a railway from Bastille to Bois de Vincennes. The viaduct fell into disrepair but in 1998 it was reinvented as the Viaduc des Arts (15–21 avenue Daumesnil), where jewellers, painters and other artisans can be viewed at their craft.

PLACE DES VOSGES

At the end of rue de Birague is the ★★ **place des Vosges** ❻❾. The square, originally called place Royale (it was renamed during the Revolution), was built from 1605–12 under Henri I; its red-and-white façades are widely praised for their restraint and elegant symmetry. The square was the core of the fashionable Marais in the 17th century, when society figures such as Madame de Sévigné, letter-writer and chronicler of life at the court of Louis XIV, lived here. In the square's less-fashionable days, from 1832 to 1848, Victor Hugo lived on the second floor of No 6, at the Hôtel de Rohan-Guéménée. In honour of the poet's 100th birthday in 1902, the city of Paris installed the **Maison de Victor Hugo** ❼⓿ (open Tues–Sun 10am–5.40pm), a museum on his life and work, at his former home.

Jewish names in the Marais

JEWISH QUARTIER

The Jewish quarter of Paris is located south of the Marais's main artery, rue des Francs-Bourgeois, in the lively area between rue du Bourg Tibourg, rue du Roi de Sicilie, rue Malher and rue des Rosiers. On rue Pavé is the **Synagogue** ❼❶, designed by art nouveau exponent Hector Guimard. This area is also home to some excellent Jewish delicatessans and kosher restaurants.

Map on page 74

Below: Madame de Sévigné
Bottom: Hôtel Carnavalet

HOTEL CARNAVALET

At 23 rue de Sévigné is the 16th-century ★★ **Hôtel Carnavalet** ⓻. The building's present name comes from the distortion of the name of one of its former owners, Françoise de Kernevenoy. Madame de Sévigné lived here from 1677 until her death in 1696. All that remains today of the original Renaissance building are the portal on the street and the heavily restored façade of the Corps de Logis in the Cour d'Honneur (Courtyard of Honour). The courtyard contains the only statue of the Sun King to have survived the revolution.

Since 1880 this *hôtel particulier* (private mansion) has housed the **Musée de l'Histoire de Paris** (Museum of the History of Paris; open Tues–Sun, 10am–5.40pm). Its important collection documents the development of the city from its germination until the present day.

MUSÉE COGNACQ-JAY

Nearby, at 8 rue Elzévir, is the Hôtel Donon, home to the **Musée Cognacq-Jay** ⓽ (daily except Mon 10am–5.40pm). The museum contains a splendid collection of 18th-century paintings, furniture and *objets d'art*, bequeathed to the city by the founders of La Samaritaine department store. In the 16th-century building are several painted roof-beams dating from shortly after its completion.

MUSEE PICASSO

Next en route is the **★★★ Musée Picasso** , housed in the Hôtel Salé, at 5 rue de Thorigny (open daily except Tues 9.30am–5.30pm, till 6pm in summer). This *hôtel* (the name *salé* derives from the salt tax once levied by its former owner) was built in the mid-17th century. A museum dedicated entirely to the work of Pablo Picasso was moved here in 1985; thanks to a donation in lieu of death duties by the heirs of the great Spanish painter, the French state possesses 200 of his paintings and over 300 sketches and etchings, along with numerous sculptures, ceramics, collages and reliefs. All of Picasso's artistic phases are clearly documented here, and 50 works from his private collection (including paintings by Braque and Cézanne) are also on display.

ARCHIVES NATIONALES

Housed in the former Hôtel de Soubise at 60 rue des Francs-Bourgeois is the **Musée de l'Histoire de France** (open daily except Tues 1.45–5.45pm), the main collection of which is the **Archives Nationales**, the largest national archive in the world. François de Rohan, Prince of Soubise, purchased the Hôtel de Clisson with money he received from Louis XIV after having allowed His Majesty to spend several happy hours with his attractive wife. Conversion of the *hôtel* was entrusted to Pierre-Alexis Delamair, a previously unknown pupil of Mansart. Only the main portal remains of the original building. The high point of any visit to the magnificent interior is the oval salon, a masterpiece of the rococo style.

MUSÉE DE LA CHASSE

In rue des Archives is the **Hôtel Guénégaud**. Constructed in 1648–51, it is the only building in Paris that can actually be proved to be the work of the great architect François Mansart (1598–1666). The façade of the building, which today houses the **Musée de la Chasse et de la Nature** (Museum of Hunting and Nature), is noticeably restrained.

Star Attractions
- Hôtel Carnavalet
- Musée Picasso

Cirque d'Hiver
Just west of the Marais, at boulevard du Temple, is the Cirque d'Hiver, a neoclassical edifice built in 1852 to a design by the Cologne architect Hittorf. The building has since been converted into a multi-purpose hall, and can accommodate up to 6,000 people. The famous Bouglione circus family has a long-term lease on the building, but numerous other events also take place here.

Musée de la Chasse et de la Nature

11: Montmartre

A separate village from Paris until 1860, Montmartre ('Martyr's Hill') is located to the north of the city, elevated on the highest hill in Paris. According to legend, St Denis, the first bishop of Paris, was decapitated on the site of the Chapelle du Martryr (11 rue Yvonne-Le-Tac) in AD287; the bishop coolly picked up his head and carried it to where the basilica of St-Denis now stands. By the end of the 19th century artists including Toulouse-Lautrec made Montmartre their home; Utrillo, Modigliani and members of the Ecole de Paris followed. Cubism was born here, with Picasso's *Les Demoiselles d'Avignon* painted in a studio in the Bateau Lavoir. By the 1920s, high rents had forced many up-and-coming artists south to Montparnasse, but many studio buildings remain, and some of them are occupied by artists.

Some parts of the area (place du Tertre and around the Sacré-Coeur basilica, the neo-Byzantine chalky white dome of which crowns the *butte,* or hill) are overly busy with tourists, especially

Map below

Cimetière Montmartre
Located just west of rue Lepic is the Cimetière Montmartre. The graves reflect the artistic bias of the local residents in this area of Paris. Famous names buried here include: composers Jacques Offenbach and Hector Berlioz; writers Alexandre Dumas, Heinrich Heine, Stendhal (Henri Beyle) and Théophile Gautier; and film director François Truffaut, buried here in 1984. A bust dedicated to Emile Zola is on show in the cemetery, although his body is now in the Panthéon.

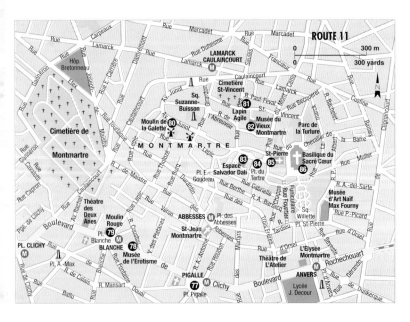

in summer, but venture off the main drag, down steep, narrow, cobbled side streets, and you should be able to experience the romanticism of Montmartre for yourself.

PIGALLE

When the artists migrated to less expensive Montparnasse in the 1920s, the area at the base of the hill was taken over by sex-shop owners, pawnbrokers and sleazy hotels. Nowadays, Pigalle (from 'Pig Alley', as American soldiers called the area) is still Paris's red-light district, dominated by tacky strip joints and seedy sex shops.

Below: the Lapin Agile
Bottom: the Moulin Rouge

From **place Pigalle** ❼ you can either walk up the hill or take the **Montmartrain**. This tourist train (departs Apr–Oct, 10am–7pm, every 30 minutes, and Nov–Mar, 10.30am–6pm, every hour) offers a tour of the whole area in 40 minutes, allowing you to hop on and hop off as you wish.

Pigalle is an appropriate venue for the **Musée de l'Erotisme** ❼ (72 blvd de Clichy, open daily 10am–2am, www.eroticmuseum.net), a collection of erotic art from all over the world. Close by is the ★★**Moulin Rouge** ❼, identifiable by its huge red sails. In 1896 this was the scene of the first fully nude striptease – the 'dancer' was arrested and imprisoned, and students protested in the Latin Quarter. Feather-clad can-can girls still perform several shows a night here but it's mostly for the tourist market nowadays.

MOULIN DE LA GALETTE TO LAPIN AGILE

From the Moulin Rouge, turn right onto rue Lepic, towards Montmartre proper, then right into rue des Abbesses. The metro at Abbesses is one of only two in the city (as well as Porte Dauphine) that still has its original art nouveau glass awning designed by the exponent of that style, Hector Guimard. Van Gogh lived at No 56 between 1886 and 1888. Next left is rue Tholozé, where you can see the **Moulin de la Galette** ❽. Renoir's masterpiece *Bal au Moulin de la Galette* catapulted the Moulin, then an inn and dance hall, to stardom.

Art nouveau

Influenced by the fluidity of natural forms and the innovative British arts and crafts movement, art nouveau was initially developed in the early 1890s by Belgian architect/designers such as Victor Horta and Henry van der Velde, who designed La Maison de l'Art Nouveau in Paris from which the style took its name. It is particularly associated with the work of Hector Guimard (1867–1942), well-known from his iconic designs for the Paris Metro – the entrance at Abbesses, in Montmartre, is especially fine.

Near here is the romantic square Suzanne-Buisson, where St Denis – rather less delightfully – is said to have washed his head after he had been decapitated; a statue commemorates the gruesome event. The elegant avenue Junot, just by here, is home to many artists' studios; No 15 was especially designed for the Romanian Dadaist poet Tristan Tzara by the Austrian architect Alfred Loos.

The corner formed by rue des Saules and rue St-Vincent is one of the area's most picturesque corners. The hill was once a wine-growing area and covered in vines; nowadays, only the last few grow in a vineyard on this spot, but every autumn, when the grapes are harvested, the vineyard here becomes the centre of a wine festival.

Opposite rue des Saules and rue St-Vincent is the cabaret known as the **Lapin Agile** ㉛, or Agile Rabbit. Once a meeting-place for Picasso, Renoir, Utrillo and Verlaine, it is still a busy venue. It owes its name to the artist A. Gill, who painted his name and a rabbit on the inn-sign.

MONTMARTRE'S MUSEUMS

Slightly further south is rue Cortot, where, at No 12, an artists' community once flourished. Renoir, Utrillo and Raoul Dufy all had studios in the 17th-century manor house here. The building's former garden-house has been converted into the **Musée**

The inspiration for Montmartre-based film, Amélie

du Vieux Montmartre ㉜ (open daily except Mon 11am–6pm), dedicated to showing the work of the former residents. The museum's star exhibit is Toulouse-Lautrec's poster, *Le Moulin Rouge*, in which Louise Weber (known as La Goulue, or the Glutton) dances the can-can.

Another exhibition space in the area is the **Espace Salvador Dalí** ㉝ (11 rue Poulbot; open daily 10am–6pm), dedicated to work of the eccentric Spanish artist. Very few of his main pieces are on show, except in reproduction, and the entrance fee is rather inflated.

AROUND PLACE DU TERTRE

Head south down rue du Mont Cenis towards **place du Tertre** ㉞, Montmartre's old village square. Delightful in erstwhile days, the square now shows the worst side of Montmartre – it's tourist orientated, with artists poised to paint your caricature, restaurants charging vastly inflated prices, and shops selling tacky tourist souvenirs.

Just a few steps away is **St-Pierre-de-Montmartre** ㉟, one of the oldest churches in the city, founded by Louis VI in 1133.

SACRÉ COEUR

At the highest point of the *butte* is the imposing ★★ **Sacré Coeur** ㊱ (open daily 9am–7pm). The Catholic basilica was founded as a national church of expiation after the French lost the war against Prussia in 1871. Construction work began in 1875, to designs by architect Paul Abadie; work was slow, however, and when the basilica was finally finished in 1914, the outbreak of World War I delayed its consecration until October 1919.

The Sacré Coeur is a cruciform, centrally planned building in the form of a square, with a high main dome and four smaller subsidiary domes. The broad, high interior (110m/360ft long, 50m/165ft wide) is dominated by the enormous, Byzantine-style mosaic of Christ in the apse.

The *parvis* or square in front of the church affords one of the best views of Paris.

Star Attraction
● **Sacré Coeur**

Below: Musée du Vieux Montmartre
Bottom: Sacré Coeur

Map
opposite

Cruising the canals

Cruises along the Canal de l'Ourcq to La Villette leaves from the quai de la Loire, parallel to the bassin de la Villette, and are organised by **Canauxrama** (13 quai de la Loire; tel: 01 42 39 12 00) and **Paris Canal** (19 quai de la Loire; tel: 01 42 40 96 97). To return, cruises depart daily at 2.30pm, from the red-enamelled Folie des visites du Parc (see opposite) at La Villette.

Along the Parisian canals

12: The Northeast

Canals conjure up images of cities such as Venice and Amsterdam rather than Paris, but to the northeast of the French capital's city centre there is an extensive network of waterways that were built by Napoleon to channel water into Paris. In the 19th century warehouses were erected along parts of the canal to cope with the massive growth in freight haulage, but by the 20th century de-industrialization and the development of road haulage caused the area to fall into decline. Since the late 1980s, however, regeneration has taken off here, and the canals, which lead up to La Villette, the largest park in Paris, are now used for recreational purposes. Also in the northeast are Belleville and Ménilmontant , two areas incorporated into Paris in 1860; although traditionally poor, both are becoming increasingly fashionable and are known as bohemian areas with a diverse cultural mix and lots of good ethnic restaurants.

ALONG THE CANALS

If you want to walk the route, start at **République**, from where it's a pleasant canalside stroll to La Villette; alternatively, make your way up the canal by boat *(see box, left)*. If you're walking, head along rue du Faubourg du Temple then take a left onto the **Canal St-Martin**; walk along quai de Jemmapes and quai de Valmy, to the **Rotonde de la Villette ③**; this rotunda was built as a tollhouse in the 18th century at the southeastern end of the harbour of the **Bassin de la Villette ③**. Warehouses and cafés around the harbour cater mainly to the leisure boaters, although some of the industrial space has been reclaimed by artists as studio space. Just beyond the port, the canal divides into Canal St-Denis and Canal de l'Ourcq, two working waterways.

PARC DE LA VILLETTE

The Canal de l'Ourcq runs into the ★★ **Parc de la Villette** (Métro Porte de Pantin, Porte de la Villette; open daily except Mon). Built on the site of a huge abattoir, which was rendered obsolete by improved refrigeration techniques and poor design (the cows couldn't even get up the steps), 55 hectares (135 acres) of futuristic gardens surround a huge science museum, a music musem, several cinemas and other cultural attractions.

The gardens of the park are the largest to be built in Paris since Haussmann's time. Designed by landscape architect Bernard Tschumi and opened in 1993, they comprise several thematic areas such as the Jardin des Frayeurs Enfantines (Garden of Childhood Fears), with a huge dragon slide, and the Jardin des Vents (Garden of Winds), home to multicoloured bamboo plants. Abstraction continues in the form of Tschumi's *folies*: red, angular tree houses minus the trees, each with a special function such as play area, workshop, daycare centre or café.

Star Attraction
● **Parc de la Villette**

SOUTH OF THE CANAL

The former cattle market now houses a cultural and conference centre in the immense 19th-century **Grande Halle ⑧**. This is the only remaining hall

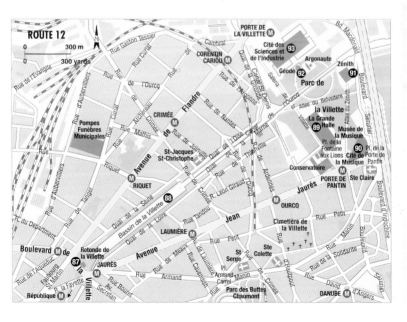

Map
on page
89

of three that once stood on this site: the central, Grande Halle was used for cattle, calves were slaughtered for veal in the eastern hall, and lambs were killed in the western hall. An additional hall was built in 1874 for pigs. The last cow was slaughtered here in 1974, and Grande Halle is now used for art fairs, catwalk shows and other events.

The other buildings in the south of the park are focused on music. Next door to the Grande Halle is the **Cité de la Musique ⑨⓪**, designed by Christian de Portzamparc. It houses a music and dance conservatory, a concert hall and the **Musée de la Musique** (open Tues–Sat noon–6pm, Sun 10am– 6pm; closed Mon; www.cite-musique.fr), charting the development of classical, jazz and folk music and housing over 4,500 musical instruments. Further east is the **Zénith ⑨①** concert hall.

Below: la Cité des Enfants
Bottom: la Géode

NORTH OF THE CANAL

This part of the park is home to the polished-steel spherical ★★ **Géode ⑨②** (open Tues–Sun 10am– 9.30pm, closed Mon; www.lageode.fr), an enormous hollow steel ball composed of 6,433 stainless-steel triangles and measuring 36m (118ft) in diameter. The Géode contains one of the largest wrap-around screens in the world . Nearby are **L'Argonaute**, a retired naval submarine and **Cinaxe**, a stomach-churning flight-simulator-cum-cinema.

Reflected in the Géode's shiny steel is the ★★ **Cité des Sciences et de l'Industrie** ㉓ (Tues–Sat 10am–6pm, Sun 10am–7pm, closed Mon; www.cite-sciences.fr), a state-of-the-art, highly interactive museum of science and industry. Begin at *L'Univers* with a spectacular planetarium and explanation of the inexplicable Big Bang. *La Vie* is an eclectic mix of medicine, agriculture and economics. *La Matière* reproduces a nuclear explosion, and *La Communication* has displays of artificial intelligence, three-dimensional graphics and virtual reality. The Cité des Enfants is aimed specifically at children.

Next to the Cité des Sciences is a small space called **Maison de la Villette**, home to a permanent exhibit on the history of La Villette.

BELLEVILLE AND MÉNILMONTANT

To the south of La Villette, in the area known as **Belleville**, is the **Parc des Buttes-Chaumont** (Métro Botzaris, Buttes-Chaumont), built by town planner Baron Haussmann in the 1860s on the site of a rubbish dump and gypsum quarry. The uneven ground provided a perfect setting for a wooded, rocky terrain, and a lake has been created around an artificial 50-metre (165-ft) 'mountain', capped by a Roman-style temple, with a waterfall and a cave containing artificial stalactites. Ice-skating, boating and donkey rides are also on offer, and the puppet show or 'Guignol' in the open-air theatre has been going for 150 years.

South of Belleville is Ménilmontant, home to the largest graveyard in Paris, the **Cimetière du Père Lachaise** (20 boulevard du Ménilmontant; open daily 9am–5.30pm). Named after Louis XIV's confessor, the Jesuit Père de la Chaise, this is one of the most illustrious resting places in Paris. Among those buried here are the medieval lovers Abélard and Héloïse, Bellini, Bizet, Chopin, Edith Piaf and Jim Morrison, whose grave has become a shrine for his fans, Delacroix, Ingres, Balzac, Beaumarchais, Colette, Molière, Proust, Oscar Wilde (note his elaborate grave by sculptor Joseph Epstein), Sarah Bernhardt and Yves Montand.

Star Attractions
- Géode
- Cité des Sciences et de l'Industrie

👁 *Les grands projets*
François Mitterrand initiated the following renovation and building projects, known as '*les grands projets*', thus ensuring his mark be left on the city:
- Renovation of the Louvre (1981–97); building of I.M. Peï's pyramid
- Cité des Sciences, La Villette (1986)
- Institut du Monde Arabe (1987)
- Gare d'Orsay conversion to a museum (1986)
- Grande Arche, La Défense (1989)
- Opéra Bastille (1989)
- Finance ministry, Bercy (1989)
- Bibliothèque Nationale de France, new buildings at Tolbiac (1998)

François Mitterrand

Map
below

In the Cimetière
de Montparnasse

13: Montparnasse

This formerly hilly area to the southwest of the centre was christened Mount Parnassos (after the home of Apollo and his muses) in the 17th century. Around the turn of the 20th century the area became a magnet for artists and writers including Chagall, Léger, Soutine and Picasso who decamped from Montmartre due to the latter's inflated rents. The establishment known as **La Ruche** (The Beehive) at 52 rue de Dantzig became famous as a meeting-place for the arty crowd, and cafés such as Le Dôme, La Coupole, La Rotonde and Dupont were frequented by Russian émigrés including Lenin and Trotsky, and composers such as Stravinsky.

Between the two world wars Montparnasse was the meeting-place for many writers who would later achieve worldwide fame, such as Ernest Hemingway, Henry Miller, André Gide, Paul Verlaine,

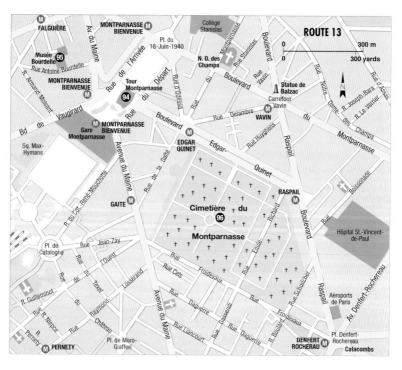

Louis Aragon, Jean-Paul Sartre and Simone de Beauvoir. The Closerie des Lilas (171 boulevard de Montparnasse) was among their favourite haunts.

Nowadays, attractions in the area are limited to cafés, the soaring Tour Montparnasse, a sculpture museum and one of Paris's main cemeteries.

TOUR MONTPARNASSE

After World War II city planners began an ambitious redevelopment project, the most visible symbol of which is the Maine-Montparnasse skyscraper, right outside Montparnasse station. At 210-m (690-ft) high, ★ **Tour Montparnasse 94** (summer, daily 9.30am–10.30pm; 56th and 59th floors only) was the highest in Europe when completed in 1973. The foundations had to be rammed 70m (230ft) into the earth to support the building's 120,000-ton weight. Fifty-two floors house offices, and the entire edifice uses up as much power as a town with 30,000 inhabitants. From the restaurant on the 56th storey and the roof terrace there are superb views of Paris and, in good weather, much of the Ile de France. The lift takes just one minute to reach the top.

Behind the tower is the **place du 18 Juin 1940**, named in commemoration of the day on which General de Gaulle, in a radio message from London, urged the French to resist the Germans : 'We have lost a battle, but not the war.'

ADDITIONAL SIGHTS

At 16–18 rue Antoine-Bourdelle is the **Musée Bourdelle 95** (open daily except Mon 10am–5.40pm), a showcase for the work of the sculptor Antoine Bourdelle (1861–1929). A pupil of Rodin, Bourdelle is known for his modernist friezes on the Théâtre des Champs-Elysées. The artist's former studio and apartments are open to visitors.

The **Cimetière de Montparnasse 96**, the third largest graveyard in Paris (18 hectares/14.5 acres), was laid out in 1824. Among those buried here are the sculptors François Rude and Antoine Bourdelle and the writers Baudelaire, Guy de Maupassant, Jean-Paul Sartre and Simone de Beauvoir.

> **The catacombs**
> After a walk through the graveyard, a visit to Les Catacombes (open Tues–Fri 2–4pm, Sat and Sun 9–11am and 2–4pm) should not be missed. The catacombs are situated at the place Denfert-Rochereau, beneath the Métro station of the same name. There were subterranean quarries here in Gallo-Roman times. After the cemeteries in the city centre were closed in 780, around 6 million skeletons were brought here. The bones are piled up in the galleries along the winding passageways. Danton and Robespierre were supposedly buried here, and it was the Resistance headquarters during World War II.

Inside the catacombs

Versailles

Spend one day at ★★★ **Versailles**, France's third most-visited monument, and you should be able to see the château's main buildings plus the gardens, all described here. (Palace: open Tues–Sun May–Sept 9am–6.30pm, Oct–Apr till 5.30pm. Grand and Petit Trianon: open daily Nov–Mar noon–5.30pm, Apr–Oct noon–6.30pm. Coach Museum: Mar–Nov, Sat and Sun 2–5pm only. Gardens: open daily except in very poor weather, Apr–Oct open 7am, Nov–Mar open 8am, closed 5.30–9.30pm depending on season.)

Below: corridor at Versailles
Bottom: the palace from the
rear gardens

THE PALACE

For visiting purposes, the château is split into several areas. The main part includes the lavish **State Apartments** of the King and Queen (Grands Appartements), notably the King's State Bedroom in which the monarch's every move was scrutinised by his courtiers. Also in this section is the vast **Hall of Mirrors**, the ultimate glass corridor where the Treaty of Versailles was signed, signifying the end of World War I. The best time to visit the gallery is the afternoon, when the sun streams in.

Other highlights of this main tour include, in the **Hercules Room**, the ceiling painting *The Apotheosis of Hercules* (1733–6), by François

Lemoyne, and, in the Battle Gallery, a copy of the imposing *Crowning of the Empress Josephine at Notre-Dame* (1804) by Jacques-Louis David.

For a supplement – beware, there are charges for most 'extras' at Versailles – access is granted to Louis XIV's private bedroom and the **apartments of the Dauphin and Dauphine**. There are also tours of the private apartments of Louis XV, Louis XVI and the Opera; the Opera and Royal Chapel; the apartments of Madame de Pompadour and Madame du Barry; and Marie Antoinette's suite.

THE TRIANONS AND HAMEAU

The two other main buildings on the estate are the **Grand** and **Petit Trianon**, both located to the northwest of the main château. If you don't fancy the 30-minute walk, take the miniature train that runs regularly from the château, along the Grand Canal and across to the Trianons and back. Bicycles and horse-drawn carriages may also be hired in the grounds.

Marie Antoinette's **Hameau**, a cluster of thatched cottages, is northeast (10 minutes' walk) of the Petit Trianon. The official Versailles guide-books stress that these rustic-style buildings were not erected, as popularly believed, so that the Queen could play at being a shepherdess, but as a dairy where food for the estate was produced.

THE GARDENS AND PARK

If you've had your fill of architecture and interior decoration, head for the château's **gardens** and **park**. These are the work of André Le Nôtre, who grappled with narrow hillocks and marshland to create the ultimate formal-style French playground for Louis XIV.

A main feature in the park is the **Grand Canal**, an artificial ornamental stretch of water that covers 45 hectares (110 acres) and can be explored by boat. Around the canal is a network of pathways, fountain basins, hidden groves studded with statuary based on classical and mythological figures, and painstakingly sculpted trees and bushes.

Star Attraction
● Palais de Versailles

Beating the queues
Each section is entered via a different ticket office but you only have to queue once so join the shortest queue and visit that part of the château first. Smart customers pre-book at www.chateauversailles.fr.

Louis XIV

Fontainebleau

The seat of sovereigns from Louis IX to Napoleon III and a glittering example of French Mannerism, the château at ★★ **Fontainebleau** makes a pleasant day trip from Paris. It was here that the Revocation of the Edict of Nantes was signed by Louis XIV in 1685, and Napoleon I signed his first act of abdication in 1814. More recently (1945–65), Fontainebleau made its mark as the headquarters of the military branch of NATO.

Below: the monogram of François I
Bottom: the view from the grounds

BACKGROUND

Although a castle stood on the site of the present château as early as the 12th century, it was not until the reign of François I (1494–1547) that the estate really evolved. Keen to make the most of the dense forest in the Fontainebleau area for hunting, François transformed the existing buildings into a grand Mannerist palace. Henri IV (1553–1610) carried on the good work, adding the wing housing the Deer Gallery, Diana Gallery (built for his wife, Marie de Médicis), the Dauphin's entrance and the buildings around the Kitchen Courtyard.

Renovation and additions continued under monarchs from Louis XIV (1638–1715) to Louis XVI (1754–93), but with the latter came the Revolution and a bleak period for Fontainebleau, as the palace was stripped of its contents and left to ruin. Napoleon's reign proved more favourable. By 1803, he had founded a military school here and in 1804 began full refurbishment, mostly in the then-fashionable Empire Style. Napoleon also converted the Small Apartments for his personal use.

After the Restoration, Louis Philippe (1773–1850) continued to renovate the château, refurbishing much of the interior. Napoleon III (1808–73) carried on Louis Philippe's work, and the Empress Eugénie (1826–1920) had new salons installed and opened a Chinese Museum in the Great Pavilion. Note that access to some areas (Small Apartments, Napoleon Museum and Chinese Museum) is limited; call ahead on 01 60 71 50 70 to check times.

Giverny

Claude Monet lived at ★★ **Giverny** from 1883 until his death in 1926. Although none of his original paintings is on display here, visitors come to see the gardens immortalised in his art.

The house is entered through the light-drenched *atelier* (now a gift shop) in the back, where Monet painted his vast canvases of water lilies. The interior of the house is full of Japanese furniture, prints and ceramic vases, and his precious collection of Japanese engravings covers the walls of several rooms. Along with his gardens, the prints were a major source of inspiration. Most of the original furniture has disappeared and the blue and yellow dining room is a reconstruction. The most appealing room is the kitchen, with its row of copper pots and yellow crockery that Monet designed himself.

The two gardens, Le Clos Normand and Le Jardin d'Eau, are linked by a subterranean passage. The former is more traditional and rectangular, inspired by formal 18th-century designs, with archways of climbing plants and rows of bluebells, pink peonies, roses, nasturtiums, poppies and hibiscus.

The Water Garden, formed by a tributary of the Epte, lies further away, shaded by weeping willows. Here, you can see the celebrated Japanese Bridge and the lily pond.

Star Attractions
- Fontainebleau
- Giverny

Waterlilies
'It took time for me to understand the lilies', wrote Monet. 'I had planted them for pleasure; I cultivated them without a thought to painting them…then, suddenly, I experienced the revelation that there were magic worlds in my pond. I grabbed my palette and since then it is the only thing that I paint.'

Monet's Japanese Bridge

Architecure

Very little remains of Merovingian (481–751) and Carolingian (751–987) Paris, bar the Tour de Clovis (part of the Merovingian abbey of St-Pierre-et-St-Paul) and elements of the crypt of the Basilique St-Denis. The founding of St-Germain-des-Prés dates back to 543, but the earliest parts still extant are Romanesque. These, and the choir of St-Martin-des-Champs, are the only structures to have survived from that time.

THE GOTHIC

Things all changed abruptly with the development of a new architectural style in the Ile-de-France. The first plan for a Gothic structure was designed by Abbot Suger for the choir of St-Denis (construction work began in 1140). Structural innovations, originating elsewhere, such as the pointed arch and the ribbed vault, were now combined to create the new Gothic style.

The Early Gothic cathedral of Notre-Dame (1163), while less representative than Reims or Chartres outside of Paris, is still a good example of the style. It has a long, high nave, and the west façade has three doors, surrounded by statues and reliefs, topped by two towers.

In the mid-13th century the most magnificent examples of High Gothic were erected in Paris: the transept of Notre-Dame with its fine tracery, and the superb interior of the Sainte-Chapelle, commissioned by Louis IX to house his reliquaries.

THE RENAISSANCE

Francis I (1515–47) introduced Italian Renaissance forms, and the adaptation of the Gothic tradition to antique pillars and cornices resulted in a typically French façade style. Italian forms were used to create artistic and elegant surface decoration, while walls remained emphatically flat, windows high and narrow, and the steep Gothic roof, in particular, was retained in preference to the Italian flat one.

> **Place des Vosges**
> Commissioned by Henri IV and built 1605–12, this symmetrical square is made up of a series of main buildings with low wings set around a courtyard; these buildings are divided off from the street by walls, with gardens at the back. Unpretentious façades of this type gave rise to the style of house widespread in France, with its walls of red brick and its white stone corner angles and window surrounds, beneath a steep slate-grey roof.

Opposite: the Pompidou Centre
Below: Sainte-Chapelle's stained glass

Baron Haussmann
The layout of contemporary Paris owes much to Napoleon III's chief town planner, the Prefect Baron Georges-Eugène Haussmann (1809–91), who was responsible for reorganising Paris in the late 19th century. He gutted and boldly rebuilt the centre, installing new water mains and a sewage system, and replaced narrow medieval roads with a network of wide boulevards (the *grands boulevards*), which improved traffic flow and made crowd control much easier.

Notre-Dame's rose window

From 1528 construction work commenced on the palace at Fontainebleau, and from 1547 onwards the new Palais du Louvre, designed by Lescot and with fine façade reliefs by Jean Goujon, was built on the site of the previous fortress.

THE BAROQUE AND NEOCLASSICISM

In the first half of the 17th century 60 new monasteries and 20 churches were built, with the aim of turning Paris into a second Rome. These included some of France's most important religious structures: the Jesuit Church of St-Paul-St-Louis, the Church of the Sorbonne by Lemercier, and Val-de-Grâce by Lemercier and François Mansart. They were modelled on the Roman baroque church, with a two-storey gabled and pillared façade, a broad, barrel-vaulted nave flanked by chapels, and a high cupola above the crossing.

French art entered its classical phase during the reign of Louis XIV (1643–1715), most notably with the Palace of Versailles (1671), which grew to become the biggest palace in Europe. Louis Le Vau, Hardouin-Mansart and Charles Lebrun designed the buildings and André Le Nôtre laid out the magnificent formal gardens.

The same team were appointed to oversee changes to the city. The city walls were removed, and broad avenues (boulevards) took their place. The city gates were replaced by triumphal arches. Both place des Victoires and place Vendôme were redesigned as royal squares and provided with statues as centrepieces, the Louvre was extended, and the addition of the Tuileries and the Champs-Elysées created a 'Royal Axis'.

THE 19TH CENTURY

The storming of the Bastille in 1789 marked the start of the destruction of many church buildings during the years of revolution. However, Napoleon continued the tradition of the Royal Axis, extending it by adding the Arc de Triomphe.

A combination of neglect and incredibly rapid urban growth had made Paris more than ripe for redevelopment. Under Baron Haussmann *(see box, left)* the residential quarter of the Cité was pulled down, the existing street system was transformed, and parks were laid out on the outskirts of the city. Garnier's Opéra (1860–75) is a magnificent example of bourgeois architecture of the Second Empire. Victor Baltard's Halles Centrales – the earliest example of modern iron architecture in Paris – were built next to it. Further iron structures were created for international exhibitions, among them the Eiffel Tower (1889).

THE 20TH CENTURY AND BEYOND

Modernist building in Paris saw some notable designs by Le Corbusier, as well as Zehrfuss's UNESCO headquarters. During the 1970s, under Pompidou, new architectural projects included the Centre Pompidou, the Tour Montparnasse and the skyscraper suburbs of La Défense, Front de Seine and Place d'Italie. The first phase of construction on the Forum des Halles was completed, and the Marais underwent redevelopment. Building projects begun under Giscard d'Estaing (La Villette and Orsay) were completed by Mitterrand, who also commissioned larger-scale projects such as the extension of the Louvre with the glass pyramid, the Opéra Bastille, the Grande Arche at La Défense and the Bibliothèque François Mitterand.

Below: the Grande Arche at La Défense
Bottom: the mark of the father of art nouveau

Painting

Early surviving paintings in France mostly follow the dictates of the international Gothic. Outstanding works include pieces by artists Henri Bellechose, François Clouet and Jean Fouquet.

The Baroque period (*c*1600–1790) saw a flowering of French painting. Marked by a grandeur and emotional intensity, and the decorative works of the Rococo (exemplified by the paintings of Watteau, 1684–1721, Boucher, 1703–70 and Fragonard, 1732–1806), Baroque paintings exude vitality. Early artists include Georges de la Tour (1593–1652) and Nicolas Poussin (1594–1665). This was also the age of the great landscape painter Claude Lorrain (1600–82), who produced idealised views of nature influenced by the Roman countryside.

Below: The Card Cheat *(c1635–40) by Georges de la Tour* *Bottom:* Mme Récamier *(1805) by François Gérard*

NEOCLASSICISM TO REALISM

Towards the end of the 18th century the late-Baroque and Rococo gave way to Neoclassicism. Central to this development was Jacques-Louis David (1748–1825), whose portraits of Napoleon and Marat immortalised these heroes of the Revolution. David was followed in this severe style by Jean-Auguste Ingres (1780–1867), who became a fierce opponent of Romanticism.

France was not immune from the lure of this genre of painting, however, and two artists in particular, Théodore Géricault (1791–1824) and Eugène Delacroix (1798–1863), produced wildly romantic and stirring pictures. This idealist and, often, orientalist Romanticism was rejected in the works of the Realist painters Jean-Baptiste Corot (1796–1875) and Gustave Courbet (1819–77).

IMPRESSIONISM AND FAUVISM

By the second half of the 19th century artists had begun to consider an analytical method of recording light and colour, and the result was Impressionism. The use of small dabs of colour broke down the convention of line – a move that outraged traditionalists – and, in its extremest form, led to

Pointillism. Prominent Impressionists included Pierre Auguste Renoir (1841–1919), Camille Pissaro (1830–1903), Claude Monet (1840–1926) and Edgar Degas (1834–1917). Two artists who exhibited with, and had close affinity with the Impressionists, were Paul Gaugin (1848–1903), whose later work moved towards Symbolism, and Henri Toulouse-Lautrec (1864–1901), well-known for his depictions of everyday Parisian life.

The group of artists dubbed 'les fauves' (the wild beasts), from their violent use of colour, were led by Henri Matisse (1869–1954), a student of the symbolist painter Gustave Moreau (1826–98).

THE 20TH CENTURY

Although the foundations of modernism were now laid, it was Cubism, with its radical representations of three-dimensional objects on two-dimensional planes, that paved the way for later abstraction. The most towering figure of Cubism was Spanish-born Pablo Picasso (1881–1953), who moved to Paris in 1901. This trend, of artists flocking to the city from all over the world, has characterised much of the art scene in Paris up to the present day.

The painters that gathered in the city up to World War II are known as l'Ecole de Paris. They include Dada artist Marcel Duchamp (1887–1968), credited with founding conceptual art, the mystical

Manet and Cézanne
Both Edouard Manet (1832–83) and Paul Cézanne (1839–1906) have been associated with the Impressionists — a connection that is only appropriate in part. Manet did adopt the techniques of the Impressionists after 1870, but this was a departure from his earlier works, which showed off a ferocious technique with a concentration on light and shade. His depiction of controversial subjects shocked the mostly conservative art critics.

Cézanne — who has been called the greatest painter of the 19th century — did exhibit in the first Impressionist exhibition of 1874, but he is set apart from the Impressionist school by his intellectual rigour and insistence on the unity and equal importance of colour and form.

Manet's controversial
Déjeuner sur l'herbe

Russian painter Marc Chagall (1887–1985), and the Italian Amadeo Modigliani (1884–1920).

The contemporary scene in Paris is also international. Numerous galleries exhibit contemporary work, including shows by French artists Véronique Boudier, Claude Closky and Natacha Lesueur.

Below: grave of Emile Zola
Bottom: the Bibliothèque
François Mitterrand

Literature

Over the centuries Paris has acted as a magnet for writers, a breeding ground for intellectual thought, and a subject of inspiration in itself. Early written work to depict Parisian life includes the story of tragic 12th-century lovers, Abélard and Héloïse, in which the brutality of life in fiercely Catholic medieval Paris is vividly described.

The poetry of François Villon (1431–*c*.1463) takes an equally rough approach. In his bawdy poems the erstwhile vagabond Villon describes an unattractive city rife with depravity and crime. Even in the later writings of the satirical François Rabelais (1483–1553), the capital fares poorly (he slates such eminent institutions as the Sorbonne).

THE 17TH TO 19TH CENTURIES

The 17th century is considered the Golden Age of French drama. Its sons include Pierre Corneille (1606–84), Molière (1622–73), who penned plays

with strong social commentaries, and Jean Racine (1639–99), who reinvented the Classical tragedies.

By the first half of the 19th century, the city of Paris took centre stage again, lifted to almost iconic status in the hefty tomes of novelist Honoré de Balzac (1799–1850). His vast production of over 90 short stories and novels, including Paris-based *Le Père Goriot* and *Cousine Bette*, was written slavishly to order from his Parisian garret. Victor Hugo (1802–85) had his first big success with *Notre-Dame de Paris* (1831), and such was the influence of the novel that it sparked the great cathedral's long-awaited restoration in the 19th century. The poet Charles Baudelaire (1821–67) credits his explorations of the French capital as the inspiration for the prose poem, first seen in his *Spleen de Paris* of 1860; rugged yet adaptable, this new medium best reflected the shock of living in such a large city. Parisian-born Emile Zola (1840–1902) set his *Ventre de Paris* around the Halles market district, the 'underbelly of Paris' of the title. His *L'Assomoir* reveals the poverty and squalor below the glamour of Second Empire Paris, while in *Bel-Ami* Guy de Maupassant follows a provincial determined to succeed in corrupt Third Republic Paris.

THE 20TH CENTURY AND BEYOND

In the 20th century St-Germain and Montparnasse became known for their literary links. Paris continued to provide intellectual inspiration to French writers, from Surrealist André Breton and *nouvelle vague* writers such as Raymond Queneau *(Zazie dans le Métro)* to the Existentialists Jean-Paul Sartre, Simone de Beauvoir and Albert Camus. After World War I an influx of writers from outside France also moved to Paris, and the influence of their time there is seen in novels such as *Down and Out in London and Paris* (George Orwell), *A Moveable Feast* (Ernest Hemingway) and *The Autobiography of Alice B. Toklas* (Gertrude Stein).

Later French authors writing on their capital include 'Paris noir' Léo Malet (1909–96), Georges Simenon (1903–89), creator of the detective Maigret, and crime-writer Daniel Pennac (1944–).

French cinema
The moving image was invented in France by the Lumière brothers, who made their first film in 1855. Generations of directors, from Jean Cocteau, Louis Malle and François Truffaut to Jean-Luc Besson and Mathieu Kassovitz, have been beguiled by the photogenic and romantic qualities of the French capital. After World War II, the city was seen as iconic in American films such as *Funny Face* and *An American in Paris*. Although now portayed in a range of lights, the city is often shown as the home to troubled or oddball characters, whether in the tragic *Les Amants du Pont-Neuf, the* dark 1980s' *Subway, the* gritty *La Haine*, or the nostalgic, sugary-sweet *Amélie*.

Poster for the film Jules et Jim

Music

Paris has a long and distinguished musical history. Of the early composers working in and around the city, many were under the patronage of the court. These include: Josquin Desprez (1440–1521), one of the finest composers of the High Renaissance; the bass viol virtuoso Augustin Saint-Colombe (1630–1701); his pupil Marin Marais (1656–1728); and Marc-Antoine Charpentier (1640s–1704), who collaborated with Molierè and was employed at the court of Louis XIV.

Below: Stravinsky fountain
Bottom: classical music posters

THE BAROQUE TO SYMBOLISM

Three of the most notable Baroque composers were based in Paris. Louis Couperin (1626–61) is largely remembered for his keyboard music, much of which is in a fiercely contrapuntal style. His contemporary, Jean-Baptiste Lully (1632–87), was court composer to Louis XIV, and his output reflects this position, mostly comprising court entertainments such as ballets and operas. The younger composer Jean-Philippe Rameau (1683–1764) is remembered for both his keyboard works and operas, and his controversial theoretical work *Traité de l'harmonie* ('Treatise on Harmony').

After the death of Rameau, music in France underwent a slight hiatus until the appearance

of Hector Berlioz (1803–69). In many ways embodying the Romantic ideal in both his music and personal life, Berlioz was revolutionary in his approach to form and orchestration. Following in the Romantic footsteps of Berlioz were the grand opera composers Gounod, Bizet, Massenet and Meyerbeer, all of whom were closely associated with either the Paris Opéra or Opéra Comique.

The ground work for a further musical revolution was laid by the late-19th century composers, Saint-Saëns, Fauré and Dukas. Said by Pierre Boulez to be 'the beginning of modern music', *L'apres midi d'un faune* (1894) by Claude Debussy (1862–1918) brought a new sense of harmonic, rhythmic and formal freedom to music. These techniques, owing something to the influence of Impressionism and Symbolism and drawing on modal traditions, are also to be found in the early works of Maurice Ravel (1875–1937).

THE 20TH CENTURY AND BEYOND

The watershed for French music in the 20th century is marked by two events: the first performance of Igor Stravinsky's *Le sacré de printemps* in Paris in 1913, and World War I. The violence and rhythmic intensity of Stravinsky's work forced composers to rethink their approach to music, while the destruction wrought by the war made the music of the pre-war *belle époque* seem singularly inappropriate for the contemporary world.

Following the lead of Stravinsky, Ravel and the highly individual Erik Satie (1866–1925), the group of composers known as *Les Six* (Auric, Durey, Honegger, Milhaud, Poulenc and Tailleferre) produced works that might broadly be described as 'neoclassical', by imposing modernist techniques on to classical forms. These pieces drew greatly on the influence of jazz, which gave them a rhythmic vitality and contemporary flavour.

Later composers of the 20th century include Olivier Messaien (1908–1992), who drew on his mystical Catholicism and bird song in his colourful music, and his pupil Pierre Boulez (1925–), a seminal figure in the post-war *avant garde*.

> ### Chanson
> Wiith their roots in night-clubs and the music hall, French *chansonniers* seem to exemplify the chic yet sleazy Parisian nightlife of the popular imagination. Singers such as Juliette Gréco, Charles Aznavour, Yves Montand, Maurice Chevalier, Charles Trenet and, above all, Edith Piaf, projected an enduring image of the fragile but tough sentimentalist, whose songs veer between angst and frivolity.

The 'Little Sparrow', songstress Edith Piaf

FOOD AND DRINK

Although Paris is viewed by the French as the gastronomic capital of the country, it does not have its own cuisine. Breakfast *(petit déjeuner)* usually consists of a *croissant* and a cup of milky coffee *(café crème – or a grand crème* or *petit crème*, depending on how large a cup you want); lunch *(déjeuner)* and dinner *(dîner)* tend to be substantial meals. A small meal *(souper)* after a theatre visit is quite common.

FRENCH CUISINE

Traditionally, a French menu starts with soup *(potage* or *soupe)*, and in some restaurants this will be served automatically before a starter or *hors d'oeuvre*. Particularly good first courses include *oeufs en meurette* (eggs poached in red wine), smoked salmon *(saumon fumé)* and that famous Burgundian speciality, snails *(escargots)*, served with pungent garlic butter and lots of bread. Oysters *(huîtres)* are served alongside other seafood and not treated as a luxury.

Meat plays a large role in French cuisine, with the most common varieties being lamb *(agneau)*, beef *(boeuf)*, pork *(porc)* and chicken *(poulet)*. The French like their meat fairly rare, especially when it is grilled or roasted. When ordering a steak, note that *bleu* is hardly shown the fire, *saignant* is very pink, and *à point* is medium; you can also ask for well done *(bien cuit)*. Popular dishes include *boeuf bourguinon* (beef in red wine), *rognons à la moutarde* (kidneys in mustard sauce) and *andouillettes* (offal sausages).

A selection of cheeses *(fromages)* may be offered before, or instead of a dessert – not after the dessert as is the tradition in Britain. Popular sweets include *mousse au chocolat, crème brûlée, poire Belle Hélène* (pear in chocolate sauce), *île flottante* (whipped egg white in a vanilla-custard sauce), *tarte tatin (*upside-down caramelised apple tart), charlottes, tarts and other pastries.

BARS, BRASSERIES AND BISTROS

The small café-bars on almost every street corner in Paris are usually styled as a bar or brasserie and sometimes even as a café. Bistros provide breakfast, simple morning and evening snacks, such as toasted ham-and-cheese sandwiches *(croque-monsieurs)*, and all kinds of drinks.

RESTAURANTS

Parisian restaurants – of which there is a vast range to suit all tastes and purses – normally have *prix fixe* (fixed-price) menus, which represent good value but offer limited choice. Prices often include a service charge *(service compris)*, but if you have been served well, it is common to leave an additional tip.

The following selection comprises four categories: €€€€ = luxury, €€€ = expensive, €€ = moderate, € = inexpensive. It is still possible to enjoy a good three-course lunch for 8 euros.

Drinks

A French meal is usually accompanied by wine. In smart restaurants, it is a good idea to follow the recommendation of the staff, while in more modest establishments, the house wine (*vin* or *cuvée de la maison*) is usually a safe bet. Mineral water and beer *(bière)* are increasing in popularity. Also typical is an apéritif before the meal, while after dinner you may be offered a *digestif*.

Alain Ducasse au Plaza Athéné, 25 avenue Montaigne, 8th, tel: 01 53 67 65 00. For a very special occasion, you can't beat this exquisite restaurant – the first recipient of six Michelin stars. Reservations essential. €€€€

Allard, 41 rue St-André des Arts, 6th, tel: 01 43 26 48 23. Haute cuisine served amid a traditional atmosphere near place St-Michel. €€€

Angelina's, 226 rue de Rivoli, 1st, tel: 01 42 60 82 00. Famed Parisian tearoom that is also good for lunch. Great squishy meringues. €–€€

L'Apparemment Café, 18 rue des Coutuers-St-Gervais, 3rd, tel: 01 48 87 12 22. Stepping inside this quaint café near the Musée Picasso is like entering someone's house. Cosy seats make for lovely lazy dining, and the food is simple but tasty. €–€€

L'Arpège, 84 rue de Varenne, 7th, tel: 01 45 51 47 33. This fashionable restaurant near the Musée Rodin has chic modern décor and offers creative cooking and a good wine list. €€€

Astier, 44 rue Jean-Pierre Timbaud, 11th, tel: 01 43 57 16 35. A modern bistro in the north of Paris that does home cooking with an inventive touch and at a very good price. €

Au Pied de Cochon, 6 rue Coquillière, 1st, tel: 01 40 13 77 00. This famous old Les Halles market brasserie is open 24 hours a day for onion soup, pigs' trotters and seafood. €€

Aux Fins Gourmets, 231 boulevard St-Germain, 7th, tel: 01 42 22 06 57. Come here for classic French cuisine, especially *cassoulet* (white bean and meat stew), the house speciality. Buzzing bistro atmosphere. €€

Brasserie Bofinger, 5–7 rue de la Bastille, 4th, tel: 01 42 72 87 82. This classic brasserie, with stunning art nouveau décor, is claimed to be the oldest in the city. Specialities include foie gras, seafood (*fruits de mer*), and choucroute. €€–€€€

Brasserie Flo, 7 cour des Petites Ecuries, 10th, tel: 01 47 70 13 59. A wood-panelled Alsatian brasserie established in 1886, Flo is an old favourite serving seafood, choucroute and Alsatian beer and wine. €€

Brasserie Lipp, 151 boulevard St-Germain, 6th, tel: 01 45 48 53 91. Once a haunt of Jean-Paul Sartre and Simone de Beauvoir, this brasserie in the heart of smart St-Germain remains popular with the cognoscenti. €€

Café Beaubourg, 43 rue St-Merri, 4th, tel: 01 48 87 63 96. This designer café-cum-brasserie is in a choice spot opposite the Pompidou Centre and is perfect for people-watching. €–€€

Café de la Paix, 12 boulevard des Capucines, 9th, tel: 01 40 07 30 20. With décor by opera architect Charles Garnier, the Café de la Paix is classified as an historic monument. Savour a coffee in style and enjoy the view from the terrace. €–€€

Chez Jenny, 9 boulevard du Temple, 3rd, tel: 01 42 74 75 75. This classic brasserie with 1930s décor is the place to try Alsatian specialities, including choucroute and suckling pig. €€

La Closerie des Lilas, 171 boulevard du Montparnasse, 6th, tel: 01 40 51 34 50. This Montparnasse cocktail bar was once frequented by literary lights such as James Joyce and Ernest Hemingway and it's still popular with the intellectual crowd. €€

Costes, Hôtel Costes, 239 rue St-Honoré, 75001, tel: 01 42 44 50 00. The swanky restaurant at the Hôtel Costes is a place to see and be seen, and stars and VIPs come to enjoy its fine nouvelle cuisine. €€€€

La Coupole, 102 boulevard du Montparnasse, 14th, tel: 01 43 20 14 20. A fabulous art deco brasserie, replete with waiters in black and white and a buzzing atmosphere, serving quality classics: choucroute, *steak au poivre* and huge platters of seafood. €€

Le Dôme, 108 boulevard du Montparnasse, 14th, tel: 01 43 35 25 81. One of the most popular seafood restaurants in Paris. Try the tasty *bouillabaisse* (fish stew). €€€

Fouquet's, 99 avenue des Champs Elysees, 8th, tel: 01 47 23 70 60. Fouquet's is where the Parisian 'in-crowd' come to taste Gérard Sallé's cooking. One for a special occassion. €€€€

Le Fumoir, 6 rue de l'Admiral-de-Coligny, 1st, tel: 01 42 92 00 24. Tucked away at the eastern end of the Louvre is this characterical bar, which is notable for its 3,000-book library. €

Harry's New York Bar, 5 rue Daunou, 2nd, tel: 01 42 61 71 14. Harry's was shipped over bit by bit from New York. It's supposed to be the place of origin of the Bloody Mary. €

Jules Verne, Eiffel Tower, 7th, tel: 01 45 55 61 44. Innovative chef Alain Reix has a restaurant on the second level of the Eiffel Tower, where you can mix excellent food with great views. €€€

Ladurée, 16 rue Royale, 8th, tel: 01 42 60 21 79. Another Parisian institution, where it's famously hard to catch the waiter's eye. Come here for tea and macaroons (the house speciality). €€€

Ma Bourgogne, 19 place des Vosges, 4th, tel: 01 42 78 44 64. The best thing about this restaurant is its magnificent setting under the arches of the place des Vosges. The food is pricey but you can also stop just for a drink. Good service. €€€

Maxim's, 3 rue Royale, 8th, tel: 01 42 65 27 94. A famous Parisian restaurant as known for its lush art nouveau decor as its menu. €€€

Le Munich, 7 rue St-Benoît, 6th, tel: 01 42 61 12 70. This wonderful Left Bank brasserie has traditional red velvet banquettes and is a great place for seafood platters. €

Le Pause Café, 41 rue de Charonne, 11th, tel: 01 48 06 80 33. One of several trendy café/brasseries in the Bastille. The service can be slow, but there's a nice heated terrace out the front, and the food is tasty. €–€€

Le Procope, 13 rue de l'Ancienne Comédie, 6th, tel: 01 40 46 79 00. A haunt of the 'glitterati' (Voltaire, Balzac et al) since 1686. €

Le Temps de Cerises, 31 rue de la Cerisaie, 4th, tel: 01 42 72 08 63. A modest family restaurant that does simple food at lunchtime only. €

La Tour d'Argent, 15–17 quai de la Tournelle, 1st, tel: 01 43 54 23 31. The ultimate in luxury, founded in the 16th century; gastronomy museum on the ground floor. Great views. €€€

Traditional dining

NIGHTLIFE

Paris is a city that never sleeps, with entertainment to entice whatever the time of day or night. Lists of events can be found in the daily papers or the city's weekly *L'Officiel des Spectacles* and *Pariscope* listings magazines. *Pariscope* (www.pariscope.com) also has a supplement in English. The tourist office publishes a monthly listing, *Paris Selection*, and its information service is updated weekly, tel: 08 36 68 31 12 (www.paris-touristoffice.com).

THEATRE, BALLET, CLASSICAL MUSIC

There is an excellent choice of theatre, concerts, ballet and opera in Paris. Some of the main venues are listed below:

Cité de la Musique, 223 avenue Jean-Jaurès, 19th, tel: 01 44 84 45 00. The complex at La Villette includes a concert hall.

Comédie Française, 2 rue Richelieu, 1st, tel: 01 44 58 15 15. The main national theatre, where work by French classics old and new – from Molière and Racine to Genet and Anouilh – is shown.

Opéra Bastille, 130 rue de Lyon, 12th, tel: 08 36 69 78 68. Opera and ballet are both performed at the city's 'new' opera house.

Opéra National du Palais Garnier, place de l'Opéra, 9th, tel: 08 36 69 78 68. Opera and ballet are also both shown here.

Théâtre du Châtelet, 2 rue Edouard Colonne, 1st, tel: 01 40 28 28 40. Opera, modern dance and lunchtime concerts.

Théâtre du Vieux Colombier, 21 rue du Vieux Colombier, 6th, tel: 01 44 39 87 00. Small-scale productions of classical and modern drama from the Comédie Française troupe.

CABARETS

The cabarets and major revue theatres in Paris usually do two shows a night, and three at weekends. With the big shows, the so-called *dîner-spectacle* usually begins at 8pm, and the evening meal is generally included in the price, which varies but is never cheap. 'Champagne Shows' – at which a half-bottle of expensive champagne is provided – start at 10pm and midnight.

The cabaret theatres include: the **Folies Bergères** (32 rue Richer, 9th, tel: 01 44 79 98 98), the oldest in Paris, which now shows musicals; the **Lido** (116 avenue des Champs-Elysées, tel: 01 40 76 56 10), home to the Bluebell Girls; and the **Moulin-Rouge** (82 boulevard de Clichy, tel: 01 53 09 82 82), immortalised by Toulouse-Lautrec.

NIGHTCLUBS

Paris has more than its fair share of clubs and DJ bars, with something for every musical persuasion; most *'soirées'* take place in the central areas around the Louvre, the Grand Boulevards, the Latin Quarter, the Marais and Bastille, and Montmartre and Pigalle. There are so many venues that it's only possible to introduce a small number here. For a more comprehensive range, look in Pariscope or find out more on www.zingeurs.com and www.les-teufeurs.com

Alcazar (Mezzanine), 62 rue Mazarine, 6th, tel: 01 53 10 19 99. A cool bar and even cooler DJs pull in a mixed crowd of Parisians and tourists.

Le Balajo, 9 rue de Lappe, 11th, tel: 01 47 00 07 87. Popular club with a chic crowd and both Latin and rock music.

Les Bains Douches, 7 rue du Bourg-l'Abbé, 3rd, tel: 01 48 87 01 80. These former Turkish baths are frequented by the smart set – a place to see and be seen.

Batofar, 11 quai François-Mauriac 13th, tel: 01 56 29 10 00. The top candidate for coolest club in Paris is on a barge moored across from the new Bibliothèque Nationale. Electronic and world music concerts are a prelude to all-nighters with leading DJs.

Le Divan du Monde, 75 rue des Martyrs, 18th, tel: 01 44 92 77 66. Cheap and friendly, this former café (where Toulouse-Lautrec was a regular) is now a throbbing, eclectic nightclub (R&B, Brazilian, trance, etc.); no élitist door policy or dress code.

Elysée Montmartre, 72 boulevard Rochechouart, 18th, tel: 01 44 92 45 42. Fun for all ages, with theme evenings from rock 'n' roll to salsa

Les Etoiles, 61 rue du Château d'Eau, 10th, tel: 01 47 70 60 56. This is a stylish Latino club in an old cinema. Attracts top-quality musicians and a hip crowd.

Folies Pigalle, 11 place Pigalle, 18th, tel: 01 48 78 25 56. Very popular disco in an area that never sleeps.

La Java, 105 rue du Faubourg-du-Temple, 10th, tel: 01 42 02 20 52. Latin American music in a Belleville dance hall.

La Locomotive, 90 boulevard de Clichy, 18th, tel: 01 53 41 88 88. Right next door to the Moulin Rouge, this place is mainstream and absolutely vast.

JAZZ CLUBS

The best way to enjoy the lively jazz scene on the *rive droite* is to stroll along the rue des Lombards *(Métro Châtelet)*, while, on the *rive gauche*, head for rue St-Benoît *(Métro St-Germain-des-Prés)*; both streets contain several jazz clubs and pubs. Other recommended clubs include:

Caveau de la Huchette, 5 rue de la Huchette, 6th, tel: 01 43 26 65 05 *(Métro St-Michel)*. A young clientele is attracted to the cellar jazz here. Open Mon–Fri 9.30pm–2.30am and weekends 9.30pm–3.30am.

La Chapelle des Lombards, 19 rue de Lappe, 11th, tel: 01 43 57 24 24

(Métro Bastille). 'Tropical' music in popular club. Open Thurs, Fri and Sat 10.30pm–dawn.

La Cigalle, 120 boulevard de Rochechouart, 18th, tel: 01 49 25 81 75, fax: 01 42 23 67 04. Old favourite.

New Morning, 7–9 rue des Petites Ecuries, 10th, tel: 01 45 23 51 41 *(Métro Château d'Eau)*. Taking its name from a Bob Dylan song, this venue is for aficionados. Concerts start at 9pm.

CINEMA

Paris has a high concentration of multi-screen cinemas showing the latest films, but if you'd rather see a French classic than the latest Hollywood blockbuster, there are a number of good retro and arthouse cinemas. Most of the cinemas within central Paris show films in their original language with subtitles in French (these are marked 'VO', which stands for *version originale*), though once you get out of the city centre, mainstream films are usually dubbed (marked 'VF' – *version française*). Ticket prices are reduced by up to 30 per cent on Monday and/or Wednesday. Concessions may be available for students.

Ticket agencies

Agence Spectaplus, Salle Pleyel, 252 rue du Faubourg St-Honoré, 8th, tel: 01 53 53 58 60.

FNAC Billeterie, at the FNAC stores across Paris. Bookings can also be made at: www.fnac.fr.

Virgin Megastore, 52 avenue des Champs-Elysées, 8th, tel: 01 49 53 50 00. Book by phone, tel: 01 44 68 44 08, or in person Mon–Sat 10am–12am, Sun 12pm–12am.

Kiosque, 15 place de la Madeleine, 8th, sells tickets on the day at half price. Open Tues–Fri 12.30–8pm; on Sat from 12.30pm for matinées and from 2pm for evening shows; Sun 12.30am–4pm.

SHOPPING

In a world in which shopping seems to be becoming more and more uniform, with the same international groups and luxury labels in every major city around the world, Paris can still put forward its claim to be the shopping capital of Europe. For one thing, there's an incredible variety of shops in what is a compact, beautiful and easily manageable city. Paris also retains its tradition of small specialist shops and personal attention. Although there has been a tendancy for fashion labels to try and gain a citywide spread, there are fewer chain stores here than in much of Europe. Thankfully, with the exception of the Forum des Halles and a couple of smaller shopping centres, Paris has remained largely free of the purpose-built *centres commerciaux* (shopping malls) and the rash of hypermarkets and discount stores that disfigure the Parisian suburbs and the outskirts of many provincial French cities. Instead, individual boutiques ensure that the historic heart of Paris remains a vibrant, living centre.

Most boutiques and department stores open at 9am, although some do not open until 10am; food shops – especially bakers – open much earlier than that. Traditionally in France, most shops close at noon and reopen around 2.30pm, but in Paris, many shops now remain open until 7 or 7.30pm. Many of the larger department stores are open until 9 or 10pm on Thursdays. In the suburbs, hypermarkets usually stay open until 8–9pm. Most shops are closed on Monday morning, some all day Monday.

FASHION

Paris is still the designer city of the world, and all the top-name fashion houses have boutiques here. As Calvin Klein said when he opened his avenue Montaigne store, 'It's the most important city in Europe to show the world what you do.' The top couture houses are mostly either in the avenue Montaigne area or around the Faubourg St-Honoré, while more individual boutiques cluster around the Marais and St-Germain-des-Prés.

Other main shopping areas include the rue de Rivoli, the streets around the Opéra, the grands magasins and the boulevard Haussmann. Here you'll find French chains such as Naf Naf and Kookaï and many of the large department stores. For boutiques, try the Marais and the Bastille.

Traditionally the sales *(soldes)* are held in July and January, but many shops now offer mid-season reductions.

DEPARTMENT STORES

The city has a handful of one-stop department stores including:
Le Bon Marché Rive Gauche, 22 rue de Sèvres, 7th, tel: 01 44 39 80 00, www.lebonmarche.fr. One of Paris's most stylish *grands magasins*, in a building designed by the architect Gustave Eiffel.

> ### Tax
> Most prices include TVA (value-added tax, or VAT). Foreign visitors can claim this back – worth doing if you spend over around €650 (€300 for non-EU residents) in one place. Ask the store for a *bordereau de vente à l'exportation* (export sales invoice). This must be completed and presented with the goods to customs officers on leaving France. Pack items separately for ease of access. The form is mailed back to the retailer, which refunds the TVA in a month or two. Certain goods (such as antiques) may need special clearance. For more information contact the Centre de Renseignements des Douanes, tel: 01 53 24 68 24.

Once called 'une cathédrale du commerce' (a cathedral of shopping) it sells haute couture fashions and make-up.

La Grande Epicerie de Paris, 38 rue de Sèvres, 7th, tel: 01 44 39 81 00, www.lagrandeepicerie.fr. Le Bon Marché's gourmet grocery store sells every delicacy under the sun.

bhv (Bazar de l'Hôtel de Ville), 52–64 rue de Rivoli, 4th, tel: 01 42 74 90 00, www.bhv.fr. Sells everything you'll need to meet your DIY needs. Great art department, but limited fashions.

Galeries Lafayette, 40 boulevard Haussmann, 9th, tel: 01 42 82 34 56, www.galerieslafayette.com. An entire floor devoted to lingerie and the largest perfume department in the world, beneath a breathtakingly beautiful art nouveau steel and glass dome.

Printemps Haussmann, 64 boulevard Haussmann, 9th, tel: 01 42 82 50 00, www.printemps.com. The store is housed in three buildings, each devoted to a theme: L'Homme (menswear), La Maison (home) and La Mode (womenswear).

La Samaritaine, 19 rue de la Monnaie, 1st, tel: 01 40 41 20 20, www.lasamaritaine.com. Set at the north end of Pont Neuf in a fine art deco building, this store is one of the less-flashy department stores. The rooftop café of store number 2 gives way to fantastic 360° views over Paris.

MARKETS

The city is particularly known for its markets, which offer everything from bric-a-brac to live animals.

Place Louis-Lépine, 4th. Flowers. Open daily 8am–7.30pm. Birds. Open Sun 8am–7pm.

Place de la Madeleine, East side of the church, 8th. Flowers. Open daily except Mon 8.30am–7pm.

Quai de la Mégisserie, 1st. Birds, dogs, cats and fish. Open daily 10am–7pm.

Marché d'Aligre, rue/place d'Aligre. General. Open daily, mornings only.

Les Puces de Clignancourt, Porte de St-Ouen to Porte de Clignancourt, 18th. Flea market. Open Sat–Mon, 7am–7pm.

Les Puces de Vanves, porte de Vanves–Porte Didot, avenue Georges Lafenestre, rue Marc Sangnier, 14th. Flea market. Open Sat–Sun, 7.30am–5pm. Nearby is **Marché aux Puces de St-Ouen**, open 10am–6pm for antiques.

Rue Mouffetard, 5th. Food and flowers. Open Tues, Thurs, Sat. 9am–1pm, 4–7pm. The nearby market at place Monge offers food and flowers on Wed, Fri and Sat.

Rue de Buci and **Rue de Seine**, 6th. Off Boulevard St-Germain. Food – fruit and cheese – wine and flowers. Open Tues–Sun, 8am–1pm.

Shopping philosophy

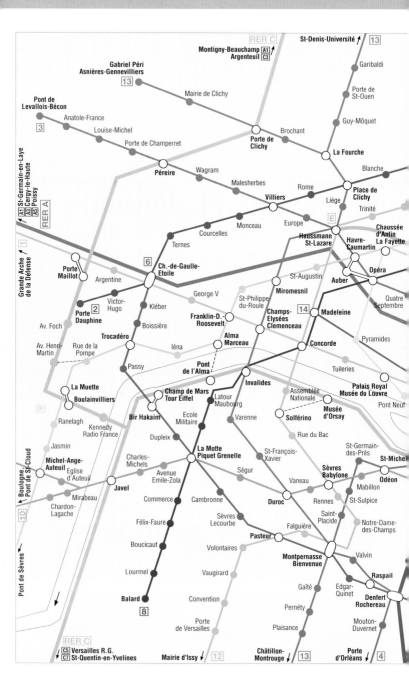

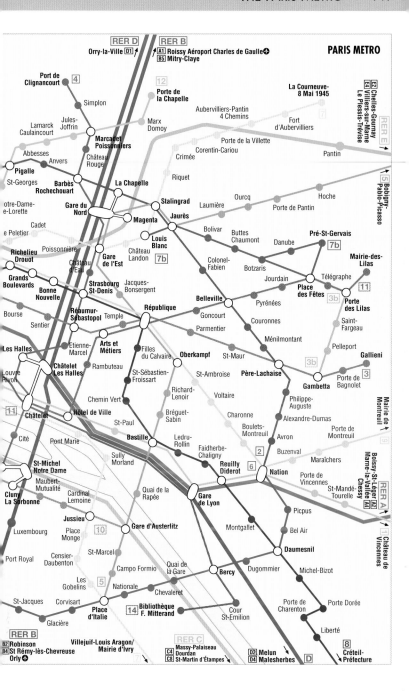

PRACTICAL INFORMATION

Getting There

BY PLANE

Most major airlines fly regularly to Paris. Air France is the main agent for flights to France from the US and within Europe (tel: 0845 0845 111) and also handles bookings for smaller operators such as Air Vendée and Brit Air. For British travellers, smaller operators (such as the low-cost airlines Ryanair, Buzz, Easyjet and British Midland) offer flights from British cities to provincial French airports.

Travellers from the US and Canada can fly direct to Paris and larger cities such as Nice and Lyon on Air France and most US airlines. For long-haul passengers, a charter flight to London then on to Paris may prove cheaper. In Paris, Nouvelles Frontières and Forum offer competitive fares on scheduled and charter flights.

Students and young people under 26 can get discount charter flights through specialist travel agencies. In the UK, try Campus Travel, 52 Grosvenor Gardens, London SW1W OAG, tel: 020-7730 3402. In the US, try USIT, New York Student Centre, 891 Amsterdam Avenue, New York, NY 10025, tel: 212-663 5435, www.usitnow.com and www.usitworld.com

Paris has two airports: Roissy–Charles de Gaulle, 23 km (15 miles) north of the city via the A1 or RN2 (tel: 01 48 62 22 80, information available in English), and Orly, 14 km (9 miles) south of the centre via the A6 or RN7 (tel: 01 49 75 15 15, information available in English).

BY TRAIN

The quickest and most convenient way of reaching Paris from London is to take the Eurostar service from Waterloo Station; Eurostar trains may also be caught from Ashford International station in Kent (tel: 01233 617575 from within the UK; 08 36 35 35 39 in France; or visit www.eurostar.com).

Tickets may be booked for through journeys from outside France. In the UK tickets can be booked from any railway station, including ferry and Channel Tunnel travel *(see below)*. There are several rail-only and rail combination passes available to foreign visitors.

In the UK: Further information on the above can be obtained from: Rail Europe, Victoria Station, London SW1, tel: 08705-848848; www.raileurope.co.uk

In the US: Contact Raileurope Inc. on their nationwide toll-free number 1-800-4-EURAIL or in **Canada** 1-800-361 7425.

BY SEA

Several ferry services operate from the UK to the northern ports of France. All of them carry cars as well as foot passengers. Hovercraft crossings are fast, but more dependent on good weather

---

Public holidays

1 January *(Jour de l'An)*, Easter Monday *(Pâques)*, 1 May *(Fête du Travail)*, 8 May *(Victoire 1945)*, Ascension, Pentecost *(Pentecôte)*, 14 July (Bastille Day – *Fête Nationale*), 15 August *(Assomption)*, 1 November *(Toussaint)*, 11 November *(Armistice 1918)*, Christmas Day *(Noël)*.

Details of public holidays are normally posted outside banks and post offices. A holiday that falls on Thursday or Tuesday causes a *pont* (bridge), where the day before or after is also taken as leave from work to make a long weekend. Many small shops and restaurants also close in August, the city's unofficial holiday month.

than the ferries. The Seacat catamaran service offers the quickest crossing but, like the hovercraft, can only carry a limited number of cars.

BY CAR

Visitors from the UK can also take **Le Shuttle**, the 35-minute Channel Tunnel service that carries cars and their passengers from Folkestone to Calais on a drive-on-drive-off system. Payment is made at toll booths, which accept cash, cheques or credit cards. You can book or just turn up and take the next available service.

If possible, a car should really only be used for arrival and departure, because Paris traffic can be extremely tricky to negotiate – Parisian drivers are renowned for their recklessness. It's also almost impossible to find anywhere to park in the city.

The fastest highways to Paris are the *autoroutes*, toll roads run by private companies. There are no special formalities for cars entering France for less than six months, but you may have to show proof of insurance, and it is wise to have international green card insurance, obtainable from your own insurance company.

Speed limits: Maximum speeds permitted in France are as follows: on motorways 130kmph (80mph), on main roads 110kmph (68mph), on country roads 90kmph (55mph), on the ring road *(Periphérique)* 80kmph (50mph) and in built-up areas 50kmph (30mph).

Breakdown service: Breakdown and tow-away services in France are well organised. Help can be obtained on motorways via the emergency telephone, and from the emergency *Police Secours* number (dial 17) on country roads and in towns and villages.

Documentation: Motorists need their car papers, driving licence and nationality sticker.

Customs

There are no limits imposed on the amount of tobacco or alcohol you can take into France if you are travelling from another EU country. (You may be required to prove at customs that the goods are for personal use only.) If you are entering France from a non-EU country, there are limits on the amount of goods you can import without paying duty – 100 cigarettes, 2 litres of wine, 1 litre of spirits, 50g of perfume, 250g of eau de toilette, and other goods up to the value of €183. Amounts in bank notes exceeding €7,600 (or equivalent) should be declared by all visitors intending to export them.

BY COACH

Eurolines, a consortium of almost 30 coach companies, operates daily services from London Victoria to Paris. This is one of the cheapest ways of reaching the city, and discounts are available for young people and senior citizens. The ticket includes the ferry crossing (via Dover) and National Express coaches have connections with the London departures from most major towns in the UK.

For details contact Eurolines UK, 23 Crawley Road, Luton LU1 1PP, tel: 01582 404511; or Gare Routière Internationale, 2 avenue Charles de Gaulle, 93541 Bagnolet Cedex, tel: 08 36 69 52 52, www.eurolines.com

TRAVEL DOCUMENTS

All visitors to France need a valid passport. No visa is currently required by visitors from any EU country, or from the US, Canada, New Zealand or Japan. Nationals of other countries do require a visa. If you intend to stay in France for more than 90 days at any one time, then a *carte de séjour* must be obtained from the French consulate – this also applies to EU members until restrictions are relaxed.

Taxis

Unoccupied taxis can be recognised by illuminated signs on their roofs. There are three tariffs (A, B and C), which relate to the time of day and area (central Paris on a weekday is tariff A). Supplements are payable for more than three passengers (most drivers will not take more than this), luggage and heavy parcels. Radio taxis can be reached at the following numbers: Alpha, tel. 01 45 85 85 85; Taxis Bleus, tel. 01 49 36 10 10; G7, tel. 01 47 39 47 39 (this company accepts credit cards over a certain amount). Remember that these cabs include the distance driven to reach customers and waiting time in their overall fares.

Getting Around

THE MÉTRO

In its early days at the beginning of the 19th century the Métro consisted of various different sections. Today the rail network, which has over 360 stations and is more than 200km (125 miles) long, is being continually extended in the suburban areas. The lines are numbered and indicators show the final stop on each line. During peak traffic hours, there is up to one train a minute. The tickets are valid for the entire Métro network, allowing passengers to travel as far as they like and change as often as they wish. The first Métro train runs at 5.30am, the last leaves at around 12.30am.

If you're staying in Paris for a few days, you have several options. Those wishing to travel extensively over the space of a few days should buy a tourist ticket (*Formule 1* and *Paris-Visite*), valid for 1, 3 or 5 days on the Métro, bus and RER lines as well as some SNCF trains. If you envisage travelling a moderate amount, buy a *carnet* of 10 single tickets – this is cheaper and more convenient than the same number of tickets bought individually.

For week-long stays, buy a *Carte Orange* (you'll need a passport-sized photo). This ticket is valid Monday to Sunday on all Métro, RER and bus lines within the city limits.

RER (RÉSEAU EXPRESS RÉGIONAL)

The lines of the RER (Express Métro) are not only useful for those wishing to cross the city in a hurry, but also for excursions into the surrounding Ile de France and to the airports. There are five main lines, A, B, C, D and E, which divide up into branch lines on the outskirts of Paris (A1, A2 etc). For clearer identification the RER trains also have names. The trains run underground in the city centre, and above ground in the suburban areas. Within the city, Métro tickets are also valid for the RER. (Note, however, that if you travel outside the city limits (for example to Roissy/ Charles-de-Gaulle or Versailles) you will have to pay more than the cost of a city-centre Métro ticket.)

BUSES

Bus stops have red-and-yellow signs, with the numbers of the various lines. Bus lines with numbers on a white background run daily, and those on a black background run Mon–Sat only. Tickets can be bought from the driver or at Métro stations, as buses accept the same tickets as the Métro. Buses run from 6.30am–8.30pm; some lines only function until 12.30pm on Sunday. Taking a bus during rush hour usually isn't a good idea because of the busy traffic.

BICYCLE HIRE

The following companies offer bicycle hire and guided tours (sometimes by night), including routes around 'undiscovered' Paris:

Paris à Vélo C'est Sympa, 37 boulevard Bourdon, 4th, tel: 01 48 87 60 01.
Paris Vélo, 2 rue du Fer à Moulin, 5th, tel: 01 43 37 59 22.

SIGHTSEEING TOURS

By bus: You can see much of the city by scheduled bus – try lines 24, 29, 32 and 38, among others. The **Balabus** covers the main sites in Paris on a 50-minute run. You can pick it up at any stop marked Balabus (Bb). Most hotels have brochures offering guided coach tours, but these tend to be more expensive than going it alone. Other firms running sightseeing tours include:

By private coach: Coach tours allow you to see Paris with minimum effort. Most companies provide a taped commentary in several languages. The main firms include:

Paris-Vision. Leaves from 214 rue de Rivoli, tel: 01 42 60 30 01.

Cityrama. Leaves from 4 place des Pyramides, tel: 01 44 55 61 00.

Les Cars Rouges are double-decker buses that stop at Trocadéro, the Eiffel Tower, Louvre, Notre-Dame, Musée D'Orsay, Opéra, Arc de Triomphe and Grand Palais. You can hop off, sightsee, then catch a later bus. The trip takes 2½ hours. Tel: 01 42 30 55 50.

By boat: Sightseeing trips by boat along the Seine are provided by several firms. They generally take 1½ hours, or 3 hours including lunch or dinner. The ships run all year round from several points along the Seine and along the canals (*see pages 57 and 88*).

Facts for the Visitor

EMBASSIES AND CONSULATES

America, 2 rue St-Florentin, 1st, tel: 01 43 12 22 22.

Great Britain, 16 rue d'Anjou, 8th, tel: 01 44 51 31 00.

Canada, 35 avenue Montaigne, 8th, tel: 01 44 43 29 00.

LOST PROPERTY

Bureau des Objets Trouvés, 36 rue des Morillons, Métro Convention, tel: 01 55 76 20 00. Open Mon–Fri 8.30am–7pm, Tues and Thurs until 8pm.

MEDICAL ASSISTANCE

Visitors from the EU have the right to claim the same health services available to the French. UK visitors should obtain form E111 from the Department of Health prior to departure. It is still advisable to have private health insurance in case of circumstances not covered by the reciprocal arrangement.

For visitors from outside the EU, the best way to guarantee problem-free medical treatment is to take out a private traveller's health insurance policy before you travel. Information is available from travel agents and health-insurance companies.

High-tech Paris underground

MONEY

The currency in France is the euro (€), which is divided into 100 cents (¢ or ct). There are coins *(pièces)* for 1, 2, 5, 10, 20 and 50 cents, and 1 and 2 euros, and notes *(billets)* for 5, 10, 20, 50, 100, 200 and 500 euros.

Banks are usually open Monday to Friday 9am–4.30pm (often closed in the afternoon on days preceding public holidays). The easiest way to obtain cash is from ATMs outside banks (DABS, distributeurs automatiques de billets) using the cashpoint or credit card issued by your home bank. Most machines accept Visa, Amex, Maestro and Cirrus. Avoid changing money in hotels where rates may be unfavourable. **Exchange counters** in SNCF rail stations are open until late

> **⧖ Emergencies**
> In the event of an emergency call:
> • Ambulance (SAMU): 15
> • Fire department (Sapeurs Pompiers): 18
> • Police: 17
> • Emergencies from a mobile: 112
> • Emergency doctors (SOS Médecins):
> tel: 01 47 07 77 77
> • Emergency dentists (SOS Dentaire):
> tel: 01 43 37 51 00
> • 24-hour pharmacy: Dhéry, 84, avenue des Champs-Elysées; tel: 01 45 62 02 41.
> In all emergencies SOS Help operates an English helpline from 3–11pm daily: 01 47 23 80 80.

(midnight at Gare du Nord, Gare de Lyon until 11pm); 24-hour money exchange is available at Orly and Roissy–Charles de Gaulle airports.

In the event of credit-card loss, call one of the following numbers:
Visa/Carte Bleue. Tel: 08 36 69 08 80
Diner's Club. Tel: 01 49 06 17 17
American Express. Tel: 01 47 77 72 00
MasterCard. Tel: 01 45 67 84 84

MUSEUMS

Museums usually close on Monday or Tuesday. Because of the huge crush to get into some museums and exhibitions, the *Réunion des Musées Nationaux* opened a shop in which museum tickets can be ordered and bought in advance in France or from abroad: Musées & Compagnie, 49 rue Etienne-Marcel.

Cartes Musées et Monuments is a pass valid for one, three or five days, allowing access to over 65 museums and sights in Paris, obtainable at the larger Métro stations and the Office de Tourisme *(see opposite)*.

POST OFFICE

The French post office is run by the PTT (Poste et Télécommunications). The main branches are open 8am–7pm on weekdays and 8am–noon on Saturday. Stamps *(timbres)* are available at most tobacconists and other shops selling postcards or greetings cards.

TELEPHONES

Most public phone boxes in Paris are card-operated. Phone-cards, or *télécartes*, can be bought from kiosks, tobacconist's and post offices. You can also make calls from post offices, which have both coin- and card-operated phones. To call long-distance, ask at one of the counters and you will be assigned a booth – you pay when your call is over. Cafés and tabacs often also have public phones, which usually take either coins or, in the case of the more old-fashioned models, *jetons* – coin-like discs bought at the bar.

All telephone numbers in France have 10 digits. Paris and Ile de France numbers begin with 01; freephone numbers begin 08 00; premium rate numbers begin 08 36 and mobile phone numbers begin 06. For French directory enquiries and the operator, ring 12; international directory enquiries is 3212.

To call other countries from France, first dial the international access code (00), then the country code: Australia 61, UK 44, US and Canada 1. It's worth remembering that you get 50 percent more call-time for your money if you ring between 10.30pm and 8am on weekdays, and from 2pm at weekends.

You cannot reverse telephone charges within France but you can to other countries where such calls are accepted. Go via the operator (12) and ask to make a *pcv* ("pay-say-vay") call.

TIME
France is six hours ahead of US Eastern Standard Time and one hour ahead of Greenwich Mean Time.

TIPPING
Most restaurant bills include a service charge, and this is generally indicated at the foot of the menu. If in doubt, ask: Est-ce que le service est compris? In any case it is common to leave a small additional tip for the waiter if the service has been good. Remember to address waiters as *Monsieur*, never as *garçon*; waitresses are *Mademoiselle* or *Madame* according to age.

It is customary to tip taxi drivers 10 percent, though this is not obligatory.

TOURIST INFORMATION OFFICES
Information and brochures are available from French tourist information/ Maison de la France offices but note that those outside Paris do not make hotel reservations.

UK: 178 Piccadilly, London W1V 0AL, tel: 0891 244123.

US: 444 Madison Avenue, 16th floor, New York, NY 10020, tel: 212-838 7657.

Canada: 1981 McGill College, Tour Esso, Suite 490, Montreal H3A 2W9, Quebec, tel: 514-288 4264; 30 St Patrick Street, Suite 700, Toronto M5T 3A3 Ontario, tel: 416-593 6427.

Toilets

In most places in Paris the old, much-feared Turkish-style public lavatories *(pissoirs)* have been replaced with pavement capsules, known as 'Sanisettes'. There is a small charge to visit these booths, but they are chemically cleaned after each visit and even offer musical accompaniment.

Lavatories in restaurants and bistros may usually be used free of charge, although sometimes there's a small fee (sometimes you have to collect a key from the manager). The larger Métro stations also have public conveniences; again, there may be a small fee for these or a tip might be expected from the caretaker.

In Paris, information may be obtained from the Office de Tourisme de Paris, 127 avenue des Champs-Elysées, 8th, tel: 08 36 68 31 12, fax: 01 49 52 53 00. Most of their information is also now on their comprehensive website *(see below)*.

VOLTAGE
220 volts AC, though 110 still exists in rare cases. An adapter for two-point sockets is needed.

WEBSITES
A wealth of tourist information is available over the net and the following is just the tip of the iceberg:

• www.paris-touristoffice.com (official tourist office site, with information on hotels, sites, events, exhibitions etc)
• www.paris.org (general information)
• www.magicparis.com (travel, shops, hotels)
• www.pariscope.com (*Pariscope* on-line)
• www.ratp.fr (the official Paris transport system site)
• www.musexpo.com (museums and exhibitions guide)
• www.france.com (general information on France)
• www.meteo.fr (the weather on-line)
• www.pagesjaune.com (the *Yellow Pages*)

ACCOMMODATION

There are around 5,000 hotels in Paris, of which about 1,400 are called Hôtels de Tourisme, which means they are regularly checked by the state and can be recognised by their dark-blue, octagonal signs with a white 'H' in the middle, outside their entrances. The letters NN *(nouvelle norme)* mean that the hotel is up to the latest tourist standards. The official French classification system has five categories, from no stars to four stars. Since hotels in Paris are at a premium, it is best to reserve a room weeks in advance.

Hotel selection

The following is a brief selection of recommended hotels ranging from deluxe (€€€€ = over 310 euros per night) to expensive (€€€ = 160–310 euros per night) to moderate (€€ = 80–160 euros per night) and inexpensive (€ = 80 euros or less per night). All prices are a rough guide to the cost of a double room with an ensuite, except for some inexpensive hotels, where you may have to share a bathroom. Breakfast is usually extra. A small amount is also charged for hotel tax.

Hôtel Beaumarchais, 3 rue Oberkampf, 11th, tel: 01 53 36 8686; fax: 01 43 38 32 86. Trendily decorated hotel that is handy for the hip Marais and Bastille areas. €–€

Chopin, 10 boulevard Montmartre, (46 passage Jouffroy), 9th, tel: 01 47 70 58 10, fax: 01 42 47 00 70. Set at the end of a 19th-century glass-and-steel-roofed arcade, this is a quiet, friendly, simply furnished hotel. €

Le Crillon, 10 place de la Concorde, 8th, tel: 01 44 71 15 01, fax: 01 44 71 15 02, www.crillon.com Built for Louis XV in the 18th century, the Crillon is one of Paris's grandest hotels, accommodating everyone from visiting royalty to film stars. Facilities include a winter garden, piano bar, fitness centre and two restaurants, Les Ambassadeurs and L'Obélisque. €€€€

De l'Abbaye, 10 rue Cassette, 6th, tel: 01 45 44 38 11, fax: 01 45 48 07 86. In this tastefully converted former abbey the public rooms are large and filled with fresh flowers, and there is a lovely conservatory-style breakfast room/bar in the old chapel with French windows out on to the courtyard garden. €€€

De l'Angleterre, 44 rue Jacob, 6th, tel: 01 42 60 34 72, fax: 01 42 60 16 93. Formerly the British Embassy, this hotel maintains a faintly English air. There is a beautiful staircase with *trompe l'oeil* murals and a lovely courtyard garden. €€

De Banville, 166 boulevard Berthier, 17th, tel: 01 42 67 70 16, fax: 01 44 40 42 77. An art deco-style townhouse with an elegantly furnished piano bar. Bedrooms are tastefully and comfortably decorated, and the service is of an old-fashioned excellence. €

De Nesle, 7 rue de Nesle, 6th, tel: 01 43 54 62 41. A laid-back student and backpackers' hotel with no advance booking, basic facilities and great, spotless bedrooms with murals, furnished to various eclectic themes. There is also a garden with a pond and an impressive palm tree. €

De Nice, 42bis rue de Rivoli, 4th, tel: 01 42 78 55 29, fax: 01 42 78 36 07. This gorgeous hotel, with antique mirrors and doors, and period engravings, prints and fabrics, is owned by collectors-turned-hoteliers. It has basic amenities but bags of character. €

De Vieux Paris, Relais Hôtel du Vieux Paris, 9 rue Gît le Coeur, 6th, tel: 01 44 32 15 90, fax: 01 43 26 00 15. This 19th-century hotel was a favourite in the 1950s and '60s with

American Beat Generation writers William Burroughs and Allen Ginsberg. Today, it is rather more luxurious and attracts a new generation of aspiring artists. €€

Duc de St-Simon, 14 rue de Saint-Simon, 7th, tel: 01 44 39 20 20, fax: 01 45 48 68 25. A lovely 18th- and 19th-century hotel just off the boulevard St-Germain, with a little secret garden and a courtyard. The salon is beautifully furnished and the bedrooms elegant yet cosy. There is no restaurant, but two famous cafés – the Deux Magots and the Café de Flore – are just nearby. €

Ducs de Bourgogne, 19 rue du Pont-Neuf, 1st, tel: 01 42 33 95 64, fax: 01 40 39 01 25. Ideally situated for the Châtelet and the Louvre, this hotel is furnished with antiques and the public rooms are warm and welcoming. Modern, well-appointed bedrooms. €€

Ermitage, 24 rue Lamarck, 18th, tel: 01 42 64 79 22, fax: 01 42 64 10 33. Tucked away behind the Sacré-Coeur, this friendly little hotel is full of surprises. Its old-fashioned parlour is decorated with antiques, prints and photographs, and walls, glass panels, skirtings and doors are painted with scenes of Montmartre by artist Du Buc. Light, spacious bedrooms with tiny bathrooms. No credit cards. €

Four Seasons George V, 31 avenue George V, 8th, tel: 01 49 52 70 00, fax: 01 49 52 70 20, www.fourseasons.com Fabulous antiques, paintings and tapestries adorn this vast, famous hotel, beautifully restored and celebrated for its lavish style. €€€

Grand Hôtel des Balcons, 3 rue Casimir-Delvigne, 6th, tel: 01 46 34 78 50, fax: 01 46 34 06 27. The wrought-iron balcony of the name fronts this art nouveau hotel. They do a hearty English breakfast. €

Grand Hôtel l'Evêque, 29 rue Cler, 7th, tel: 01 47 05 49 15, fax: 01 45 50 49 36. On a lively, market street on the Left Bank, this inexpensive hotel has been fully renovated to a decent standard. €

Jeu de Paume, 54 rue Saint-Louis-en-Ile, 4th, tel: 01 43 26 14 18, fax: 01 40 46 02 76. This 17th-century building began life as a palm-game court (the forerunner of tennis) and is now an original hotel, with stone walls, exposed beams and a glass-walled lift. It has a courtyard garden and sauna. €€

Lutetia, 45 boulevard Raspail, 7th, tel: 01 49 54 46 46, fax: 01 49 54 46 00. This lavish hotel on the Left Bank is exquisitely decorated in art nouveau style. The bar is a fashionable literary venue. €€€

Hotel reservation office
If you arrive with nowhere to stay, head for the main Paris tourist office (Office de Tourisme, 127 avenue des Champs Elysées, Métro Charles-de-Gaulle-Etoile), near the Arc de Triomphe. This huge office runs a hotel-booking service. There are also offices at the main railway stations except St Lazare. The following also offer reservation services:
Paris Séjour Réservations
Tel: 01 53 89 10 50
Fax: 01 53 89 10 59
Prestotel
Tel: 01 45 26 22 55
Fax: 01 45 26 05 14

Montalambert, 3 rue de la Montalambert, 7th, tel: 01 45 49 68 68, fax: 01 45 49 69 49. Beautifully restored hotel with fashionable bar and immaculate designer furnishings. You can choose between antique or sleek modern décor in the bedrooms. There are splendid views from the eighth floor. €€

Pavillon de la Reine, 28 place des Vosges, 3rd, tel: 01 40 29 19 19, fax: 01 40 29 19 20. Ideally located on the place des Vosges, this hotel is beautifully furnished and has a quiet courtyard. €€€

Pershinghall, 49 rue Pierre Charron, 8th, tel: 01 58 36 58 00, fax: 01 58 36 58 01, www.pershinghall.com This 19th-century house, the former World War I headquarters of General Pershing and the American Legion, is now a gorgeous luxury hotel. The 26 rooms and suites are decorated in a chic, sober yet warm manner, and the windows throughout look on to a vertical 'garden'. €€€

Hôtel Place des Vosges, 12 rue de Birargue, 4th, tel: 01 42 72 60 46; fax: 01 42 72 02 64. The best thing about this hotel is its excellent location on a quiet street just off place des Vosges.

Plaza-Athénée, 25 avenue Montaigne, 8th, tel: 01 53 67 66 65, fax: 01 53 67 66 66. This grand 19th-century Empire-style hotel close to the Théatre des Champs-Elysées is a favourite with performers and composers. €€€€

Regina, 2 place des Pyramides, 1st, tel: 01 42 60 31 10, fax: 01 40 15 95 16. Antique furnishings and art nouveau details make this gorgeous hotel by the rue de Rivoli a favourite for film sets. €€€

Relais Christine, 3 rue Christine, 6th, tel: 01 40 51 60 80, fax: 01 40 51 60 81. For calm in the midst of St-Germain, try this exquisite hotel set in the cloisters and chapel of a 16th-century abbey. €€

Ritz, 15 place Vendôme, 1st, tel: 01 43 16 30 30, fax: 01 43 16 36 68, www.ritzparis.com Built by Hardouin-Mansart for César Ritz and inaugurated in 1898, the Ritz is still the place to stay for many of the world's wealthiest people. Famed as the setting for the last supper of Princess Diana and Dodi Al Fayed. €€€€

Saint-André-des-Arts, 66 rue Saint-André-des-Arts, 6th, tel: 01 43 26 96 16, fax: 01 43 29 73 34. A late 16th-century hotel, originally built to house the king's musketeers and now sporting an old shop-front façade. In the entrance, you will find an old choir stall (complete with misericords) and a listed staircase. The warren of plain, thin-walled bedrooms are all different, but not without their charm.

St Beuve, 9 rue Saint Beuve, 6th, tel: 01 45 48 20 07, fax: 01 45 48 67 52. Discreet, cosy hotel with fireplace and country antiques in the salon, a favourite with the art scene, tastefully decorated and hung with contemporary paintings. €€–€€€

Saint-Germain, 50 rue du Four, 6th, tel: 01 45 48 91 64, fax: 01 45 48 46 22. In the heart of St-Germain, close to the Sorbonne and the Luxembourg Gardens, this hotel has a warm and friendly atmosphere and comfortable bedrooms decorated in Laura Ashley style. €€

Saint-Louis, 75 rue Saint-Louis-en-Ile, 4th, tel: 01 46 34 04 80, fax: 01 46 34 02 13. This smart, old-fashioned hotel on the Ile St-Louis has warm, rustic decor and is furnished with antiques. Great location right in the heart of the city. €

Saint-Louis-Marais, 1 rue Charles-V, 4th, tel: 01 48 87 87 04, fax: 01 48 87 33 26. The sister hotel to St-Louis-en-Ile with exposed beams, tiled floors and attractively decorated rooms. €€

Youth hostels

Cheap accommodation in Paris fills up quickly, so it's advisable to book well in advance. Paris hostels are run by several main organisations, notably the Féderation Unie des Auberges de Jeunesse (FUAJ), 27 rue Pajol, 18th, tel: 01 44 89 87 27 or 9 rue Brantôme, 3rd, tel: 01 48 04 70 40 (www.fuaj.fr), and the Ligue Française pour les Auberges de Jeunesse (LFAJ), 67 rue Vergniaud, 13th, tel: 01 44 16 78 78 (auberges-de-jeunesse.com). During university vacations, you may also be able to rent student accommodation. For further details, contact CROUS, Académie de Paris, 39 avenue Georges Bernanos, 5th, tel: 01 40 51 36 00.

☀ INSIGHT COMPACT GUIDES

Great Little Guides to the following destinations:

Algarve	Finland	Rhodes	Jersey
Amsterdam	Florence	Rio de Janeiro	Lake District
Antigua/Barbuda	French Riviera	Rome	London
Athens	Goa	St. Lucia	New Forest
Bahamas	Gran Canaria	St. Petersburg	North York Moors
Bali	Greece	Salzburg	Northumbria
Bangkok	Holland	Shanghai	Oxford
Barbados	Hong Kong	Singapore	Peak District
Barcelona	Ibiza	Southern Spain	Scotland
Beijing	Iceland	Sri Lanka	Scottish
Belgium	Ireland	Switzerland	Highlands
Berlin	Israel	Sydney	Shakespeare
Bermuda	Italian Lakes	Tahiti	Country
Brittany	Italian Riviera	Tenerife	Snowdonia
Bruges	Jamaica	Thailand	South Downs
Brussels	Jerusalem	Toronto	York
Budapest	Kenya	Turkey	Yorkshire Dales
Burgundy	Laos	Turkish Coast	
California	Lisbon	Tuscany	USA regional:
Cambodia	Madeira	Venice	Boston
Cancún & the	Madrid	Vienna	Cape Cod
Yucatán	Mallorca	Vietnam	Chicago
Chile	Malta	West of Ireland	Florida
Copenhagen	Menorca		Florida Keys
Costa Brava	Milan	UK regional:	Hawaii – Maui
Costa del Sol	Montreal	Bath &	Hawaii – Oahu
Costa Rica	Morocco	Surroundings	Las Vegas
Crete	Moscow	Belfast	Los Angeles
Cuba	Munich	Cambridge &	Martha's Vineyard
Cyprus	Normandy	East Anglia	& Nantucket
Czech Republic	Norway	Cornwall	Miami
Denmark	Paris	Cotswolds	New Orleans
Dominican	Poland	Devon & Exmoor	New York
Republic	Portugal	Edinburgh	San Diego
Dublin	Prague	Glasgow	San Francisco
Egypt	Provence	Guernsey	Washington DC

Insight's checklist to meet all your travel needs:

■ *Insight Guides* provide the complete picture, with expert cultural background and stunning photography. Great for travel planning, for use on the spot, and as a souvenir. 186 titles.

■ *Insight Museums & Galleries* guides to London, Paris, Florence and New York provide comprehensive coverage of each city's cultural temples and lesser known collections.

■ *Insight Pocket Guides* focus on the best choices for places to see and things to do, picked by our correspondents. They include large fold-out maps. More than 130 titles.

■ *Insight Compact Guides* are the fact-packed books to carry with you for easy reference when you're on the move in a destination. More than 130 titles.

■ *Insight FlexiMaps* combine clear, detailed cartography with essential information and a laminated finish that makes the maps durable and easy to fold. 133 titles.

The world's largest collection of visual travel guides and maps

INDEX